Workbook

PEARSON

Scott
Foresman

Editorial Offices: Glenview, Illinois • Parsippany, New Jersey • New York, New York
Sales Offices: Parsippany, New Jersey • Duluth, Georgia • Glenview, Illinois
Coppell, Texas • Ontario, California • Mesa, Arizona

www.sfsocialstudies.com

Program Authors

Dr. Candy Dawson Boyd
Professor, School of Education
Director of Reading Programs
St. Mary's College
Moraga, California

Dr. Geneva Gay
Professor of Education
University of Washington
Seattle, Washington

Rita Geiger
Director of Social Studies and
   Foreign Languages
Norman Public Schools
Norman, Oklahoma

Dr. James B. Kracht
Associate Dean for
   Undergraduate Programs
   and Teacher Education
College of Education
Texas A & M University
College Station, Texas

Dr. Valerie Ooka Pang
Professor of Teacher Education
San Diego State University
San Diego, California

Dr. C. Frederick Risinger
Director, Professional
   Development and Social
   Studies Education
Indiana University
Bloomington, Indiana

Sara Miranda Sanchez
Elementary and Early
   Childhood Curriculum
   Coordinator
Albuquerque Public Schools
Albuquerque, New Mexico

Contributing Authors

Dr. Carol Berkin
Professor of History
Baruch College and the
   Graduate Center
The City University of New York
New York, New York

Lee A. Chase
Staff Development Specialist
Chesterfield County
   Public Schools
Chesterfield County, Virginia

Dr. Jim Cummins
Professor of Curriculum
Ontario Institute for Studies
   in Education
University of Toronto
Toronto, Canada

Dr. Allen D. Glenn
Professor and Dean Emeritus
College of Education
Curriculum and Instruction
University of Washington
Seattle, Washington

Dr. Carole L. Hahn
Professor, Educational Studies
Emory University
Atlanta, Georgia

Dr. M. Gail Hickey
Professor of Education
Indiana University-Purdue
   University
Ft. Wayne, Indiana

Dr. Bonnie Meszaros
Associate Director
Center for Economic Education
   and Entrepreneurship
University of Delaware
Newark, Delaware

ISBN 0-328-08177-9

8 9 10-V004-12 11 10 09 08 07

© Scott Foresman 4

Contents

Summarize

Directions: Read the passage. Fill in the circle next to the correct answer.

The United States is made up of many unique landforms. These landforms are as varied as the different regions that make up the United States.

Caves are one type of landform. Mammoth Cave in Kentucky is the longest recorded cave system in the world. It has more than 300 miles of passages. Carlsbad Caverns in New Mexico is another cave system. It began forming 60 million years ago and is known for its large chambers and geological structures.

Mountains are another type of landform. The two largest mountain ranges in the United States are the Rocky Mountains in the West and the Appalachian Mountains in the East. Some of the smaller mountain ranges include the Great Smoky Mountains in Tennessee and North Carolina and the Sierra Nevada in California and Nevada.

Much of the United States coastline is made up of beaches. Some of the most popular beaches are Laguna Beach in California, Palm Beach in Florida, and South Padre Beach in Texas.

1. Which sentence best summarizes the passage?

   Ⓐ Most landforms in the United States are located in the West.

   Ⓑ The United States has several mountain ranges.

   Ⓒ There are many different types of landforms in the United States.

   Ⓓ Most landforms were formed millions of years ago.

2. Which detail does NOT contribute to a summary of the passage?

   Ⓐ One type of landform is a cave.

   Ⓑ Much of the United States is made up of beaches.

   Ⓒ The United States has a number of mountain ranges.

   Ⓓ Carlsbad Caverns began forming 60 million years ago.

3. What is the main idea of the third paragraph?

   Ⓐ The two largest mountain ranges in the United States are the Rocky Mountains and the Appalachian Mountains.

   Ⓑ The United States has a number of mountain ranges.

   Ⓒ Much of the United States coastline is made up of beaches.

   Ⓓ The United States is made up of many unique landforms.

Notes for Home: Your child learned how to summarize a passage.
Home Activity: With your child, read a short newspaper article. Have your child orally summarize the article.

Vocabulary Preview

Directions: Match each vocabulary term to its meaning. Write the number of the term on the line before the definition. Not all words will be used. You may use your glossary.

1. region
2. landform
3. mountain
4. plain
5. desert
6. canyon
7. plateau
8. boundary
9. weather
10. climate
11. precipitation
12. temperature
13. humidity
14. equator
15. elevation
16. tropical climate
17. polar climate
18. subarctic climate
19. temperate climate
20. natural resource
21. raw material
22. process
23. harvest
24. industry
25. manufacturing
26. product
27. capital resource
28. agriculture
29. conserve
30. renewable resource
31. recycle
32. nonrenewable resource
33. human resource
34. service

____ using the soil to raise crops or animals

____ deep valley with steep rocky walls

____ natural resource that cannot be replaced

____ thing we change or process so people can use it

____ natural feature on Earth's surface

____ job that a person does for others

____ amount of moisture in the air

____ form of business

____ use something again

____ weather of a place averaged over a long period of time

____ area in which places share similar characteristics

____ something in the environment that people can use

____ how high a place is above sea level

____ person who makes products or provides services

____ large, flat, raised area of land

____ something that people make or grow

____ amount of rain or snow that falls

____ use resources carefully

____ imaginary line that circles the center of Earth from east to west

____ coldest type of climate on Earth

Notes for Home: Your child learned the vocabulary terms for Chapter 1.
Home Activity: Fourteen of the vocabulary terms were not used in this activity. With your child, find the terms in this chapter and define them.

© Scott Foresman 4

Lesson 1: Regions and Landforms

Directions: Complete the chart using the landforms and descriptions in the box.
You may use your textbook.

• contains only four states • rich farmland in Arkansas and Louisiana created by Mississippi and Red Rivers • highest and lowest landforms and temperatures in United States • Mississippi, Ohio, and Missouri Rivers flow through • Appalachian Mountains run through Maine • home to deserts and canyons • mostly hilly and rocky along the Atlantic coast; good farmland to the west • Mammoth Cave system in Kentucky • some rolling hills, such as Smoky Hills in Kansas • Rocky Mountains in New Mexico and part of Texas • includes Alaska and Hawaii • bordered by four of five Great Lakes • fertile, green valleys and heavy forests • Atlantic Coastal Plain • Death Valley

Northeast Region	
Southeast Region	
Midwest Region	
Southwest Region	
West Region	

Notes for Home: Your child learned about the five regions of the United States and the landforms that are unique to each one.
Home Activity: With your child, use information from this lesson to compare and contrast the region in which you live with the other regions in the United States.

Name _____ Date _____

Lesson 2: Climate

Directions: Answer the following questions on the lines provided. You may use your textbook.

1. How are weather and climate alike? How are they different?

   _____

   _____

   _____

2. Summarize the cycle of water from oceans, rivers, streams, and lakes into the air and back to the sea.

   _____

   _____

   _____

   _____

   _____

3. What three major factors affect the climate of a place?

   _____

   _____

4. Identify and describe four basic types of climates and give an example of each.

   _____

   _____

   _____

   _____

   _____

   _____

 Notes for Home: Your child learned about the climate of the United States.
Home Activity: With your child, create a chart to record the weather in your community for a week. Discuss any climate patterns you see.

Read Inset Maps

Directions: In the spaces provided, draw a map of your classroom. Draw an inset map that shows the location of your classroom in your school. Then answer the questions that follow.

1. How does the inset map relate to the main map you drew?

_____

_____

2. What can you learn from the inset map that you could not find out from the main map?

_____

_____

3. What can you learn from the main map that you could not find out from the inset map?

_____

_____

Notes for Home: Your child learned to read inset maps.
Home Activity: With your child, use an atlas to locate a map of your state or another state that includes an inset map. Notice which cities have been shown in inset maps. Discuss why it is important for an atlas to include inset maps.

© Scott Foresman 4

Lesson 3: Regional Resources

Each of the five regions of the United States has special resources.

Directions: Classify each resource as **Renewable** or **Nonrenewable**.
Then write at least one region in which each resource can be found.
You may use your textbook.

1. livestock _____

_____

2. cotton _____

3. corn _____

_____

4. fish _____

5. timber _____

6. silver _____

7. natural gas _____

8. coal _____

9. gold _____

10. oil _____

11. sugarcane _____

12. rice _____

13. wheat _____

Notes for Home: Your child learned about the special resources of each region of the United States and the effect of these resources on industry.
Home Activity: With your child, make a list of all the human resources with whom you or your child has had contact today.

Vocabulary Review

Directions: Circle the vocabulary term that best completes each sentence. You may use your textbook.

1. A line or natural feature that divides one area from another or one state from another is a (boundary, plain, desert).

2. Manufacturing is an important (process, elevation, industry), or form of business, in the Northeast region.

3. A (region, natural resource, landform) is a natural feature on Earth's surface, such as a mountain or a river.

4. A (mountain, plateau, canyon) is a deep valley with steep rocky walls.

5. A tree is a (renewable resource, nonrenewable resource, product) because it can be replaced.

6. A pilot checks the (recycle, humidity, weather), or the condition of the air at a certain time and place, to avoid flying into a dangerous storm.

7. An area with a (tropical climate, temperate climate, subarctic climate) is usually very warm all year.

8. The warmest climates are in places nearest to the (polar climate, equator, precipitation), an imaginary line that circles the center of the Earth from east to west.

9. A (natural resource, region, capital resource) is something in the environment that people can use.

10. To (service, conserve, harvest) means to use resources carefully.

11. A (human resource, raw material, region) is something we change or process so that people can use it.

12. (Climate, Manufacturing, Temperature) is the weather of a place averaged over a long period of time.

Notes for Home: Your child learned the vocabulary terms for Chapter 1.
Home Activity: With your child, make flashcards for the vocabulary terms in this chapter. Write each term on one side of an index card or small piece of paper and the definition on the other side.

Name _____ Date _____

Vocabulary Preview

Directions: Match each vocabulary term to its meaning or description. Write the term on the line. Not all terms will be used. You may use your glossary.

immigrant	democracy	Capitol	amendment
culture	citizen	executive branch	Bill of Rights
government	Constitution	White House	passport
republic	federal	judicial branch	tax
represent	legislative branch	Supreme Court	jury

1. _____ part of the government that makes laws

2. _____ highest court of the United States

3. _____ written plan of government

4. _____ way of life followed by a group of people

5. _____ building at which the United States Congress meets

6. _____ change to the Constitution

7. _____ part of the government that interprets laws

8. _____ form of government in which citizens have a right to take part

9. _____ panel of citizens who make decisions in a court of law

10. _____ form of government in which leaders are elected to represent the voters

11. _____ to make decisions for

12. _____ part of the government that enforces laws

13. _____ system of government in which national and state governments share power

14. _____ rules that people follow and the people who run the country

15. _____ first ten amendments to the U.S. Constitution

Notes for Home: Your child learned the vocabulary terms for Chapter 2.
Home Activity: With your child, select a brief newspaper or magazine article about the United States government. Have your child highlight or circle all the vocabulary terms that appear in the article and then define them in context as you read the article together.

© Scott Foresman 4

Name _____ Date _____

Lesson 1: Americans All

Directions: Read the following descriptions and decide which culture group each one describes. Write NA (Native American), S (Spanish), or F (French). Some descriptions may apply to more than one group. You may use your textbook.

1. _____ looked for riches and new land

2. _____ may have migrated from northern Asia, the South Pacific islands, or Australia

3. _____ explored parts of present-day Florida and New Mexico

4. _____ occupied North America by the 1400s

5. _____ lived in North America long before the Europeans came

6. _____ looked for a short route by sea to Asia

Directions: Answer the following questions on the lines provided.

7. How did the United States expand its borders to include 48 of today's 50 states?

_____

_____

_____

_____

8. What makes up the culture of a group of people?

_____

_____

9. How does the motto *E pluribus unum* describe the people of the United States?

_____

_____

_____

Notes for Home: Your child learned about the backgrounds of some of the cultural groups that make up the United States.
Home Activity: With your child, discuss the cultural heritage of your family.

© Scott Foresman 4

Name _____ Date _____

Lesson 2: We the People

Directions: Complete the following fact sheet about government in the United States. You may use your textbook.

U.S. Government Fact Sheet

Name of country: _____

Type of government: _____

How government is run:

    Citizens: _____

    Leaders: _____

    _____

Written plan of government: _____

_____

How laws can be changed: _____

Number of levels of government: _____

    Level One _____

        Top Official: _____

        Responsibilities: _____

        _____

    Level Two: _____

        Top Official: _____

        Responsibilities: _____

    Level Three: _____

        Top Official: _____

        Responsibilities: _____

        _____

    Three branches of national government: _____

Notes for Home: Your child learned about levels of government in the United States and the role elected officials play at each level.
Home Activity: With your child, research and identify the names of the local, state, and national officials elected to represent you. Write them on a sheet of paper.

Read a Time-Zone Map

Directions: Answer the following questions on the lines provided.

1. What is one advantage of having time zones?

   _____

   _____

2. What does a time-zone map show?

   _____

   _____

3. What is the relationship between a time zone and its neighboring time zones?

   _____

   _____

4. Why would an airline use a time-zone map? A federal government? A person calling from New York to Hawaii?

   _____

   _____

   _____

   _____

5. How are time zones marked on a time-zone map?

   _____

   _____

6. Look at the time-zone map on p. 54. How many time zones does the United States have? What are their names?

   _____

   _____

Notes for Home: Your child learned how to read a time-zone map.
Home Activity: With your child, look at the time-zone map on page 54. Help your child locate your state. Ask your child in which time zone your state is located. Do you have friends or relatives living in other states? If so, help your child locate those states Dnd time zones.

© Scott Foresman 4

Use with Pages 56–59.

Lesson 3: The Strengths of Our Freedoms

Directions: Complete the chart by using the terms in the box to classify the rights and responsibilities of United States citizens. Some terms will be used more than once. You may use your textbook.

Pay taxes	Make the communities and country a good place to live	Obtain a U.S. passport
Have freedom of press		Respect the Bill of Rights
Vote	Have a jury trial	Speak freely
Serve on a jury	Attend school	Obey U.S. laws
Worship freely		

United States Citizens

Rights	Responsibilities

Directions: Answer the following question on the lines provided. Which right identified above is also a responsibility? What conclusion can you draw?

_____

_____

_____

Notes for Home: Your child learned about the rights and responsibilities of United States citizens.
Home Activity: With your child, discuss the most recent presidential election. In what ways can citizens exercise their rights and their responsibilities at election time?

Vocabulary Review

Directions: Choose the vocabulary term from the box that best completes each sentence. Write the term on the line provided. Not all terms will be used. You may use your glossary.

immigrant	democracy	Capitol	amendment
culture	citizen	executive branch	Bill of Rights
government	Constitution	White House	passport
republic	federal	judicial branch	tax
represent	legislative branch	Supreme Court	jury

1. An official member of a country is a _____.

2. A paper or booklet that gives a person permission to travel to foreign countries is a _____.

3. A person who comes to live in a new land is an _____.

4. A responsibility adult citizens have is to serve on a _____, or a panel of citizens who make decisions in a court of law.

5. The three levels of _____ in the United States are local, state, and national.

6. The founders of our country set up a plan for governing the nation in a document called the _____ of the United States.

7. In a _____ the leaders are elected to make decisions for those who elected them.

8. A _____ is money the government collects to pay for its services, such as building roads, parks, and schools.

9. In a _____ system of government, national and state governments share power.

10. An _____ is a change to the Constitution that is passed by Congress.

11. Food, clothing, music, art, religion, customs, and language are all examples of a group's _____.

12. The president lives and works in the _____.

Notes for Home: Your child learned the vocabulary terms for Chapter 2.
Home Activity: Have your child use each of the vocabulary terms in context to tell you about the system of government in the United States.

Vocabulary Preview

Directions: Circle the vocabulary term that best completes each sentence. You may use your glossary.

1. A (producer, consumer) is a person who makes goods or products to sell.

2. Trains provide (globalization, transportation) for the movement of goods, people, or animals from one place to another.

3. The money a business has left over after all the costs of the business are paid is the (profit, demand).

4. The development of the railroad in the 1800s was an example of (technology, economy), the development of scientific knowledge to solve problems.

5. Telephone and email are two forms of modern (transportation, communication).

6. If you choose to buy a baseball cap rather than a soccer ball, the soccer ball is your (opportunity cost, want).

7. If the (demand, supply) for a product suddenly increases, the price of the product may rise.

8. People who live in cities live in (rural, urban) areas.

9. Regions that depend on each other for goods, services, and resources are economically (interdependent, urban).

10. Something a person must have to live, such as food, is a (need, want).

11. A person who buys goods or services is a (producer, consumer).

12. The process in which a business makes something or provides services in different places around the world is (communication, globalization).

13. People who live in small towns or on farms live in (rural, urban) areas.

14. Something a person would like to have but can live without, such as a new CD, is a (need, want).

15. The United States (profit, economy) is based on a free enterprise system.

16. Some businesses (demand, barter) their goods and services in exchange for those they need or want.

17. Having a large (demand, supply) of a product can cause the price of the product to fall.

18. A (free enterprise system, globalization) is one in which businesses decide what goods to make or services to sell.

© Scott Foresman 4

Notes for Home: Your child learned the vocabulary terms for Chapter 3.
Home Activity: With your child, analyze magazine ads or newspaper sales circulars. Have your child use as many vocabulary terms as possible to describe information in the ads.

Lesson 1: The Land of Plenty

Directions: Read each sentence below. One of the completions is NOT correct. Fill in the circle next to this answer. You may use your textbook.

1. When they migrated to the Americas, Native Americans found _____.
   - Ⓐ animals, fertile soil, and wild plants
   - Ⓑ Europeans had already settled the land
   - Ⓒ different resources in different regions
   - Ⓓ ways to use their local resources and trade for resources not available nearby

2. When Europeans came to the Americas, they _____.
   - Ⓐ settled along rivers near the coast
   - Ⓑ traded with Native Americans for resources found farther inland
   - Ⓒ gave Native Americans furs, seeds, and food
   - Ⓓ realized that the greatest resource in North America was the land

3. Producing crops and raising livestock became the nation's main economic activities because settlers _____.
   - Ⓐ could rely on resources from Europe
   - Ⓑ could clear trees and set up farms
   - Ⓒ could use the crops and the animals they raised to feed their families
   - Ⓓ could sell or trade extra farm products to others

4. Throughout the 1700s and early 1800s, people continued to move westward to _____.
   - Ⓐ find more land
   - Ⓑ live in cities
   - Ⓒ raise sheep and cattle
   - Ⓓ clear land for farms

5. The growth of industry in North America _____.
   - Ⓐ resulted from the continent's vast supply of raw materials
   - Ⓑ was influenced by advances in technology
   - Ⓒ caused many farmers to leave the land to seek better jobs in factories
   - Ⓓ caused people to move to rural areas

© Scott Foresman 4

Notes for Home: Your child learned how natural resources affected the growth of agriculture and industry in the United States throughout the 1800s.
Home Activity: With your child, identify the natural resources located in the area in which you live. Brainstorm how life in your town might be different if the natural resources of your area were different.

Lesson 2: Trade Then and Now

Directions: On the lines provided, write words or phrases to complete the
following paragraphs about Lesson 2.

1. In the early history of _____, people

   _____ for the goods and services they

   _____ and wanted. _____,

   _____, and metal disks were early forms of money. In Egypt,

   people used _____ as money. The Greeks produced the first

   _____ as money. The Chinese used

   _____ money instead of coins.

2. The economy of the United States is based on the _____.

   _____ make goods or products to sell, and they set the

   _____ for those items. _____

   buy the goods or services they want. If a good or service sells for

   _____ than it cost to make or provide, the producer usually

   makes a _____ on the sale.

3. In a free enterprise economy, a system of _____ balances the

   supply of a good or service against the _____ for that item.

   Too great a supply may lead to _____ prices. On the other

   hand, a shortage of an item may lead to _____ prices for

   consumers.

Notes for Home: Your child learned how trade evolved and the basic principles of a free enterprise system.
Home Activity: With your child, look at different items that belong to him or her. Discuss reasons for your
child's choices and the opportunity cost for each purchase. Discuss whether your child made good or
poor choices.

© Scott Foresman 4

Lesson 3: Transportation and Communication

Directions: Complete the cause-and-effect chart with information from Lesson 3.
You may use your textbook.

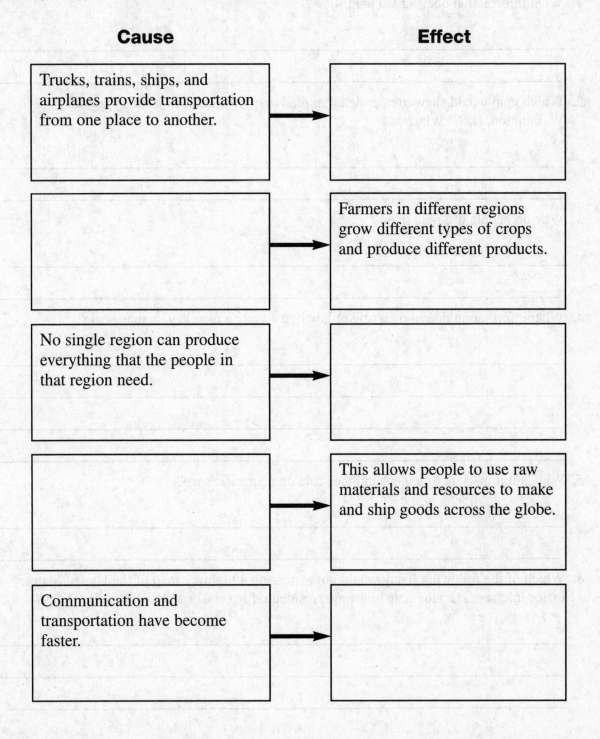

Cause	Effect
Trucks, trains, ships, and airplanes provide transportation from one place to another.	
	Farmers in different regions grow different types of crops and produce different products.
No single region can produce everything that the people in that region need.	
	This allows people to use raw materials and resources to make and ship goods across the globe.
Communication and transportation have become faster.	

Notes for Home: Your child learned how regions of the United States and other countries are interdependent.
Home Activity: Find a product manual, such as the owner's manual for an appliance. With your child, look through the manual to find the states or countries in which the components were made or assembled.

© Scott Foresman 4

Use a Road Map and Scale

Directions: Answer the following questions on the lines provided.

1. What information does a road map show?

_____

_____

2. Which map would show greater detail: a road map of Canada or a road map of Washington, D.C.? Why?

_____

_____

3. Why do people use road maps?

_____

_____

4. What information does a map title or label give you? a map key? a map scale?

_____

_____

_____

_____

5. Why is it important to understand the scale on a specific map?

_____

_____

6. Which of the following likely would not appear on a highway map of the United States: major interstates, major state highways, residential streets, or state boundaries? Why?

_____

_____

_____

Notes for Home: Your child learned to use a road map and its scale.
Home Activity: With your child, look at another road map of the United States in an atlas or in this textbook. Compare it to the map on page 86. How are the two road maps alike? different?

Vocabulary Review

Directions: Choose the vocabulary term from the box that best completes each sentence. Write the word on the lines provided. Then use the numbered letters to answer the clue that follows. Not all words will be used.

technology	barter	free enterprise system	opportunity cost
rural	producer		transportation
urban	consumer	profit	interdependent
need	economy	supply	globalization
want		demand	communication

1. Any money left over after all business costs are paid is a company's

   __ __ __ __ __ .
     2   1 12

2. An __ __ __ __ __ __ __ is how the resources of a country, state, region, or
     19

   community are managed.

3. To trade one kind of goods or service for another is to __ __ __ __ __ __ .
                       18 14

4. A person who buys goods or services is a __ __ __ __ __ __ __ __ .
               15   20 3 11

5. A person who makes goods or products to sell is a __ __ __ __ __ __ __ __ .
           10   5 9

6. The amount of an item that sellers are willing to offer at different prices is its

   __ __ __ __ __ __ .
   17   16

7. The movement of goods, people, or animals from one place to another is

   __ __ __ __ __ __ __ __ __ __ __ __ __ __ .
   7   13

8. When two regions depend on one another for goods, services, and resources, they are said

   to be __ __ __ __ __ __ __ __ __ __ __ __ __ .
       6   8   4

Clue: In what kind of economic system can businesses produce any goods or provide any service that they want?

__ __ __ __ __ __ __ __ __ __ __ __ __ __ __ __ __ __ __ __
1 2 3 4   5 6 7 8 9 10 11 12 13 14   15 16 17 18 19 20

Notes for Home: Your child learned the vocabulary terms for Chapter 3.
Home Activity: Nine of the vocabulary terms for this chapter were not used in this exercise. Have your child identify and define the terms.

Discovery
CHANNEL
SCHOOL

Use with Page 94.

UNIT 1 Project Eye on Our Region

Directions: In a group, create a video tour of your region.

1. We focused on this topic: _____

2. We made a map of our region (on a separate sheet); we included these features:

   ___cities/towns ___resources ___landforms ___interesting sights

   ___weather ___other features: _____

3. These are some interesting facts about our topic:

   #1 _____

   #2 _____

   #3 _____

   #4 _____

   #5 _____

4. We drew pictures (on separate sheets); these are the descriptions of the pictures:

   _____

   _____

   _____

✔ Checklist for Students

_____ We chose a topic about our region.

_____ We made a map of our region.

_____ We wrote facts about the topic.

_____ We drew pictures and described them.

_____ We presented our video tour to the class.

Notes for Home: Your child learned about the region in which you live.
Home Activity: With your child, research your region by using the Internet or other resources at home or at a local library. Find interesting facts or pictures that might assist your child in his or her video tour.

Sequence

Sequence means the order in which things happen.

Directions: Use what you learned about sequence to answer the questions that follow. Fill in the circle next to the correct answer.

1. Which is a clue word that can help you figure out the sequence of events?
   - Ⓐ clue
   - Ⓑ which
   - Ⓒ first
   - Ⓓ word

2. Which clue word tells you an event happened LAST?
   - Ⓐ next
   - Ⓑ finally
   - Ⓒ then
   - Ⓓ while

3. Which does NOT help you figure out the sequence of events?
   - Ⓐ clue words
   - Ⓑ times
   - Ⓒ dates
   - Ⓓ questions

4. Which clue word tells you that two events happened at the same time?
   - Ⓐ during
   - Ⓑ finally
   - Ⓒ then
   - Ⓓ next

 Notes for Home: Your child learned how to determine the sequence of a set of events.
Home Activity: Write down four events that happened recently in your child's life. Write each one on its own sheet of paper. Have your child put the events in order. Then help him or her use clue words to write or say a paragraph relating the events.

Vocabulary Preview

Directions: These are the vocabulary words from Chapter 4. How much do you know about these words? Write the number of the vocabulary word on the line next to its definition. You may use your glossary.

1. glacier

2. gorge

3. hydropower

4. hydroelectricity

5. lighthouse

6. peninsula

7. vineyard

8. bog

9. sap

10. mineral

11. quarry

12. bay

13. inlet

14. waterman

15. crab pot

_____ **a.** deep, narrow valley, usually with a stream or river

_____ **b.** area of soft, wet, spongy ground

_____ **c.** a large wire cage with several sections

_____ **d.** power that is produced by capturing the energy of flowing water

_____ **e.** place where grapevines are planted

_____ **f.** narrow opening in a coastline

_____ **g.** material that was never alive and is found in the earth

_____ **h.** place where stone is dug, cut, or blasted out for use in building

_____ **i.** tower with bright lights that shine out over the water to guide ships

_____ **j.** liquid that circulates through a plant carrying water and food

_____ **k.** part of a sea or lake that cuts into a coastline

_____ **l.** electricity produced by water

_____ **m.** huge sheet of ice that covers land

_____ **n.** piece of land almost surrounded by water, or extending far out into the water

_____ **o.** person who fishes the bay

Notes for Home: Your child learned the vocabulary terms for Chapter 4.
Home Activity: Four of the terms from this chapter are compound nouns: *lighthouse, vineyard, waterman,* and *crab pot.* Discuss with your child how these words probably were first created.

Name _____ Date _____

Lesson 1: The Beautiful Northeast

The Northeast region is one of beautiful scenery and magnificent formations.

Directions: Use complete sentences to answer the questions below. You may use your textbook.

1. What caused the formation of Niagara Falls?

_____

_____

_____

2. Why is the Niagara River important to millions of people in the Northeast?

_____

_____

_____

_____

_____

3. What are the names of at least four mountain ranges located in the Northeast region? Where are they located?

_____

_____

_____

_____

_____

4. How is the coastline of Maine different from New Jersey's coastline?

_____

_____

_____

Notes for Home: Your child learned about the different natural formations located in the Northeast region.
Home Activity: Suppose that your family is going to the Northeast to hike along the Appalachian Trail. With your child, use a map or an atlas to plan your route and discuss what items you will need to bring with you on your trip.

© Scott Foresman 4

Read a Cross-Section Diagram

A cross-section diagram shows you what you would see if you could cut through
something and then look inside.

Directions: The steps to studying a cross-section diagram can be found in the box
below. On the lines provided, write the steps in the order in which they should
occur. You may use your textbook.

Think about the terms used in the diagram.
Figure out how each part works.
Gather information from the labels on the diagram.
Look at the numbers or arrows on the diagram.
Study each labeled part of the diagram.

Step 1: _____

_____

Step 2: _____

_____

Step 3: _____

_____

Step 4: _____

_____

Step 5: _____

_____

Notes for Home: Your child learned how to read a cross-section diagram.
Home Activity: The term *cross-section* does not only refer to a diagram. Discuss with your child other
meanings of the term that he or she may have heard, such as in reference to a survey or study.

Lesson 2: Resources of the Northeast

The Northeast produces many products that people all over the world enjoy.

Directions: Suppose that you are planning a vacation to the Northeast to visit a friend or relative. Use the information from Lesson 2 to write that person a letter in which you describe some of the places you might visit, events you might attend, and the resources located there. Write your letter on the lines provided.

Dear _____,

_____

_____

_____

_____

_____

_____

_____

_____

_____

_____

_____

_____

_____

Sincerely yours,

_____

Notes for Home: Your child learned about resources of the Northeast.
Home Activity: Discuss with your child how the resources described in the text are similar to or different from resources produced in your own region or community.

Lesson 3: The Plentiful Sea

Chesapeake Bay provides seafood for people around the country.

Directions: Complete the outline with information from this lesson. You may use your textbook.

Chesapeake Bay

I. Great Shellfish Bay

A. Got its name from the Native American word _____, which means

_____

B. Rich in _____, _____, _____, other

_____, and about two hundred different kinds of _____

C. Watermen

1. Gather different kinds of _____ in different seasons

2. _____ are watermen who use _____ to capture

crabs.

II. Challenges to Chesapeake Bay

A. Pollution

1. Polluted _____ washes into rivers that drain into the bay.

2. Harms the _____ of the fish and shellfish

B. Overfishing

1. Means taking _____, _____, and

_____ from the bay faster than they can be replaced

2. Organization, _____, educates people

about the environment

Notes for Home: Your child learned about seafood found in Chesapeake Bay.
Home Activity: Making a living on the water can be very difficult, yet very rewarding. Discuss with your child the pros and cons of being a Chesapeake Bay waterman.

Vocabulary Review

Directions: Write each term on the line beside its definition.

glacier	lighthouse	sap	inlet
gorge	peninsula	mineral	waterman
hydropower	vineyard	quarry	crab pot
hydroelectricity	bog	bay	

1. _____ part of a sea or lake that cuts into a coastline

2. _____ place where stone is dug, cut, or blasted out for use in building

3. _____ deep, narrow valley, usually with a stream or river

4. _____ narrow opening in a coastline

5. _____ material found in the earth that was never alive

6. _____ area of soft, wet, spongy ground

7. _____ huge sheet of ice that covers land

8. _____ person who fishes the Chesapeake Bay

9. _____ liquid that circulates through a plant carrying water and food

10. _____ piece of land almost surrounded by water, or extending far out into the water

11. _____ large wire cage that has several sections

12. _____ place where grapevines are planted

13. _____ tower with bright lights that shine out over the water to guide ships

14. _____ power that is produced by capturing the energy of flowing water

15. _____ electricity produced by water

Notes for Home: Your child learned the vocabulary terms for Chapter 4.
Home Activity: Write a sentence that uses one of the terms above. Leave a blank where the term would be. Have your child try to fill in the missing term. Repeat for other vocabulary terms from this chapter.

Vocabulary Preview

Directions: These are the vocabulary words from Chapter 5. How much do you know about these words? Read each definition. Which word is defined? Fill in the circle next to the correct answer. You may use your glossary.

1. working together to get things done
   - (A) sachem
   - (B) convention
   - (C) import
   - (D) cooperation

2. varied
   - (A) reservation
   - (B) wigwam
   - (C) diverse
   - (D) slave

3. a fight to overthrow the government
   - (A) revolution
   - (B) export
   - (C) cooperation
   - (D) powwow

4. person who is owned as property by another person
   - (A) convention
   - (B) slave
   - (C) diverse
   - (D) import

5. a meeting held for a special purpose
   - (A) reservation
   - (B) sachem
   - (C) confederacy
   - (D) convention

6. an area of land set aside for Native Americans
   - (A) powwow
   - (B) reservation
   - (C) convention
   - (D) wigwam

7. item that is brought from abroad to be offered for sale
   - (A) import
   - (B) colony
   - (C) export
   - (D) abolitionist

8. chief of a Narragansett territory
   - (A) sachem
   - (B) abolitionist
   - (C) commerce
   - (D) wigwam

9. settlement of people who come from one country to live in another
   - (A) reservation
   - (B) diverse
   - (C) colony
   - (D) convention

10. union of groups, countries, or states
   - (A) cooperation
   - (B) confederacy
   - (C) sachem
   - (D) revolution

11. the buying and selling of goods between places
   - (A) export
   - (B) confederacy
   - (C) diverse
   - (D) commerce

12. festival of Native Americans
   - (A) powwow
   - (B) wigwam
   - (C) convention
   - (D) reservation

Notes for Home: Your child learned the vocabulary terms for Chapter 5.
Home Activity: Have your child use five of the vocabulary words correctly in a sentence.

© Scott Foresman 4

Lesson 1: The Narragansett People

The Narragansett have lived in the Northeast since before the European settlers.

Directions: Complete the web below with information from this lesson.
Then answer the questions that follow. You may use your textbook.

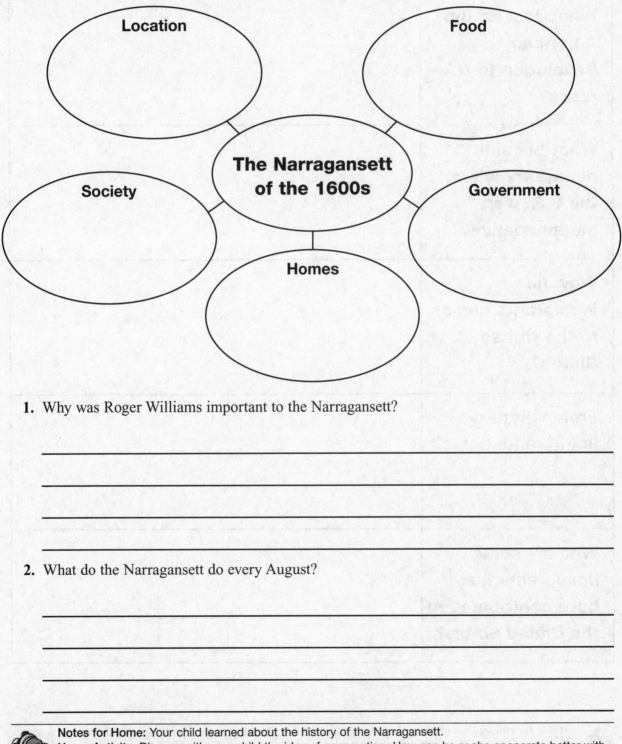

1. Why was Roger Williams important to the Narragansett?

_____

_____

_____

2. What do the Narragansett do every August?

_____

_____

_____

_____

Notes for Home: Your child learned about the history of the Narragansett.
Home Activity: Discuss with your child the idea of cooperation. How can he or she cooperate better with you and other family members? How does your family cooperate with others to meet your needs?

© Scott Foresman 4

Lesson 2: The Land of New Beginnings

Directions: Complete the chart below with information from this lesson. You may use your textbook.

What caused the American Revolution to take place?	
What became necessary when the U.S. won independence?	
Why did immigrants come to the United States?	
From where did immigrants come?	
Who are some immigrants that have contributed to the United States?	

Notes for Home: Your child learned about the American Revolution and immigration to the United States.
Home Activity: Discuss with your child to explain why our country can be called the "land of new beginnings"?

© Scott Foresman 4

Use a Vertical Time Line

A vertical time line shows events that happened over a period of time.

Directions: Complete the vertical time line below with information about the Narragansett. You may use your textbook. Information about the Narragansett can be found on pages 126–129.

Events in the History of the Narragansett

Dates	Events
1636	
1675	
1880	
1978	

Notes for Home: Your child learned how to use a vertical time line.
Home Activity: Work with your child to make a vertical time line of his or her life.

© Scott Foresman 4

Name _____ Date _____

Lesson 3: Taking a Stand

People have worked for many years to win rights in the United States.

Directions: Complete the chart below with information that explains the importance of each person or place. You may use your textbook.

Person or Place	Importance?
Philadelphia, Pennsylvania	
William Lloyd Garrison	
Frederick Douglass and Sojourner Truth	
Elizabeth Cady Stanton and Lucretia Mott	
Seneca Falls, New York	
Susan B. Anthony	

 Notes for Home: Your child learned about the abolitionist movement and the women's rights movement.
Home Activity: Discuss with your child the importance of having the right to vote. How might your child feel if, as an adult, he or she was denied the right to vote? Why?

© Scott Foresman 4

32 Lesson Review

Workbook

Name _____   Date _____

Use with Pages 140–141.

Writing Prompt: The Right to Vote

In the United States, women did not have the right to vote in national elections before 1920. Many people thought this was unfair. They did many things to try to persuade others to help women gain the right to vote. Think about why it is important for citizens to vote. Write a paragraph persuading citizens that voting is important.

_____

_____

_____

_____

_____

_____

_____

_____

_____

_____

_____

_____

_____

_____

_____

_____

Notes for Home: Your child learned about women's voting rights.
Home Activity: With your child, discuss voting and the election process. Discuss why voting is an important responsibility of citizenship.

Lesson 4: Cities Grow and Change

Northeast cities and states have undergone many changes in their history.

Directions: Read the following phrases about Northeast cities and decide which state each one describes. For a city in Pennsylvania write *PA* in the blank; for a city in New York write *NY;* for a city in Massachusetts write *MA;* write *ALL* if it describes cities in all three states. You may use your textbook.

_____ **1.** Declaration of Independence and Constitution signed here

_____ **2.** location of the Empire State Building

_____ **3.** began as a port where ocean-going ships docked

_____ **4.** became an important port on Lake Erie

_____ **5.** became centers of industry

_____ **6.** location of Paul Revere's house and Bunker Hill

_____ **7.** once famous for its steel mills

_____ **8.** headquarters for robot-making factories

_____ **9.** hub of commerce

_____ **10.** famous for its skyscrapers and its theater

_____ **11.** Freedom Trail winds past its historic sites

_____ **12.** harbor contains the Statue of Liberty

_____ **13.** passed laws to clean up the city in the mid-1900s

_____ **14.** shipping and transportation are important

_____ **15.** plentiful resources included coal and limestone

_____ **16.** center of banking, health care, and high-tech industries

© Scott Foresman 4

Notes for Home: Your child learned about the history of Northeast cities and states.
Home Activity: With your child, discuss the attractions of Northeast cities today. What might your family enjoy on a visit to these cities?

Vocabulary Review

Directions: Use the vocabulary words from Chapter 5 to complete the crossword puzzle.

Across

2. meeting held for a special purpose

3. chief or "ruler" of a Narragansett territory

5. cozy hut made of wooden poles covered with bark

7. festival of Native Americans

8. a fight to overthrow the government

9. the buying and selling of goods between different places

11. varied

13. reformer who believed that slavery should be erased from the law of the land

14. settlement of people who come from one country to live in another

Down

1. working together to get things done

4. item that is brought from abroad to be offered for sale

6. union of groups, countries, or states

8. area of land set aside for Native Americans

10. item sent from one country to be sold in another country

12. person who is owned as property by another person

© Scott Foresman 4

Notes for Home: Your child learned the vocabulary terms for Chapter 5.
Home Activity: Work with your child to write an original sentence using each of the terms above.

Name _____ Date _____

UNIT
2 Project   On the Spot

Directions: In a group, make a documentary about the experiences of early settlers or Native American groups in the Northeast.

1. We chose to make our documentary about the experiences of (✔ one):

   ____Native Americans ____European settlers

2. We included these topics:

   ____geographic location ____weather ____landforms ____homes ____activities

   ____foods available ____other groups of people ____other topics: _____

   _____

3. These are facts about the topics:

   _____

   _____

   _____

   _____

4. This is a description of our diorama or model:

   _____

   _____

   _____

✔ **Checklist for Students**

_____ We chose a group to study.

_____ We chose topics and wrote facts for the documentary.

_____ We made a diorama or model.

_____ We presented our documentary to the class.

Notes for Home: Your child learned about the experiences of early European settlers and Native Americans.
Home Activity: With your child, research the early settlers and Native Americans of your community or region. Discuss interesting facts about their experiences and their reasons for settling in the area in which you live.

© Scott Foresman 4

Main Idea and Details

A main idea is the most important thought in a paragraph. Details support, or tell more about, the main idea.

Directions: Read the paragraph. Then answer the questions that follow.

Dear Victoria,

   There is so much to do here at Myrtle Beach! We do something different every day. Yesterday, Kerry, Mom, Dad, and I went to an amusement park. Mom and Dad rode a few rides, but Kerry and I rode all of them. Today, we played miniature golf. I thought Dad would win, since he is a golfer, but I won. I got a hole in one on the last hole! Tomorrow, we are going to play in the ocean. We are having such a great time! I am looking forward to seeing you when I get home.

Your friend,

Amy

---

1. What is the main idea of the paragraph?

  Ⓐ Amy went to an amusement park.

  Ⓑ There are not many things to do at Myrtle Beach.

  Ⓒ Amy's dad is a golfer.

  Ⓓ There are many things to do at Myrtle Beach.

2. Which sentence from the paragraph is a detail that supports the main idea?

  Ⓐ Mom and Dad rode a few rides, but Kerry and I rode all of them.

  Ⓑ I thought Dad would win, since he is a golfer, but I won.

  Ⓒ We do something different every day.

  Ⓓ I got a hole in one on the last hole!

3. Which statement is NOT a detail that supports the main idea?

  Ⓐ Amy is looking forward to seeing Victoria.

  Ⓑ Amy and her family went to the amusement park.

  Ⓒ Amy and her family played miniature golf.

  Ⓓ Amy and her family plan to play in the ocean.

 Notes for Home: Your child learned how to find the main idea and details in a paragraph.
Home Activity: With your child, read an article in a newspaper or magazine. Help him or her pick out the main idea and supporting details.

Vocabulary Preview

Directions: Choose the vocabulary word from the box that best completes each sentence. Write the word on the line provided. You may use your glossary.

barrier islands	hurricane	extinct
wetlands	hurricane season	pulp
fall line	endangered species	fossil fuel
key		

1. A(n) _____ is a violent storm that forms over the ocean.

2. A(n) _____ is a material that is formed in the earth from the remains of plants or animals.

3. The _____ is a line that marks the boundary between the Piedmont and the coastal plains.

4. A low island is a(n) _____.

5. Islands formed from deposits of sand and mud are _____.

6. _____ is a combination of ground-up wood chips, water, and chemicals.

7. Lands that are at times covered with water are _____.

8. A kind of animal or plant that is thought to be in danger of dying out is a(n) _____.

9. The period from June until the beginning of November when hurricanes usually occur is called the _____.

10. About a dozen kinds of animals that live in the Everglades are in danger of becoming _____, or no longer existing.

Notes for Home: Your child learned the vocabulary terms for Chapter 6.
Home Activity: With your child, make flash cards of the vocabulary terms. Illustrate a term on one side of the card and write its definition on the other side. As you show your child each picture, have him or her spell and define the corresponding term.

© Scott Foresman 4

Lesson 1: Coastal Plains to the Mountains

Directions: Read the following statements. Then write *T* (True) or *F* (False) on the line before each statement. If the answer is false, correct the underlined term or terms to make the statement true. You may use your textbook.

_____ 1. Most of the states of the <u>Southeast</u> lie along the Atlantic coast, the coast of the Gulf of Mexico, or both.

_____

_____ 2. Off the shore are groups of long, low <u>streams</u>.

_____

_____ 3. The Outer Coastal Plain is very <u>hilly</u> and has a very <u>high</u> elevation.

_____

_____ 4. Swamps, bogs, and marshes are different kinds of <u>wetlands</u>.

_____

_____ 5. The soil of the <u>Piedmont</u> is sandy.

_____

_____ 6. The <u>Blue Ridge</u> marks the boundary between the Piedmont and the coastal plains.

_____

_____ 7. The <u>Appalachian Mountains</u> are rugged and steep, with narrow valleys.

_____

_____ 8. <u>Mount Mitchell</u> in North Carolina is the highest peak east of the Mississippi River.

_____

_____ 9. Appalachia is known for its rich natural resources, such as <u>steep valleys</u>.

_____

Notes for Home: Your child learned about the coastal plains and the mountains in the Southeast.
Home Activity: With your child, look in an encyclopedia, a magazine, or online to find a picture of a place in the Southeast. Together, discuss in which part of the Southeast you think the picture was taken. Ask your child to point out characteristics that led him or her to this conclusion.

© Scott Foresman 4

Read Elevation Maps

Directions: Fill in the blanks with information about the elevation map below. You may use your textbook for additional information.

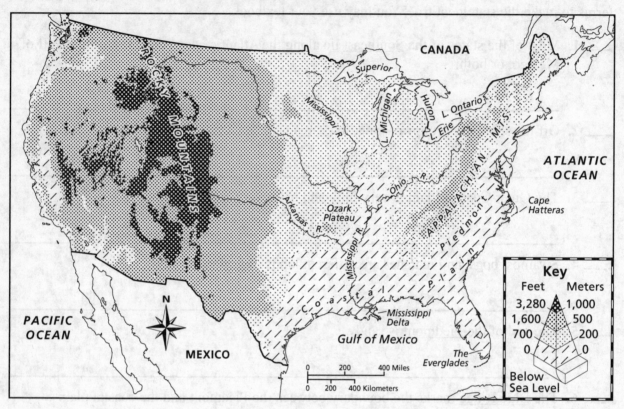

1. To read an elevation map, first look at the map _____.

2. This elevation maps uses _____ to show elevation.

3. Elevation is the height above _____.

4. A place that is at sea level is at the same _____ as the surface of the ocean's water.

5. Most of the Southeast is at what elevation range? _____

6. What is the elevation range of the highest part of the Appalachian Mountains?

_____

7. The state of Florida is entirely at what elevation range?

_____

Notes for Home: Your child learned how to read elevation maps.
Home Activity: With your child, use the map above to find the elevation of one of the physical features such as the Coastal Plain. Have your child explain how he or she used the map key to find this elevation.

Lesson 2: Sunlight and Storms

Directions: Answer the following questions on the lines provided. You may use your textbook.

1. What is Key West?

_____

_____

2. Describe the climate of Florida.

_____

_____

_____

3. What is a hurricane?

_____

_____

4. How can a hurricane affect communities in its path?

_____

_____

_____

5. Why were lighthouses originally built?

_____

_____

_____

6. Are lighthouses as important today as they once were? Explain.

_____

_____

_____

Notes for Home: Your child learned about the climate of the Southeast.
Home Activity: Have your child draw a lighthouse or examine a picture of a lighthouse. Together, discuss why lighthouses were designed to look the way they do.

Lesson 3: Wildlife and Resources

Directions: The first column of the chart below lists some of the wildlife and resources found in the Southeast. Complete the chart by writing at least one specific part of the Southeast in which each can be found.

Wildlife and Resources	Where Is It Found?
alligator	
Florida panther	
black bear	
deer	
oranges, grapefruits, lemons, limes	
peanuts	
rice	
coal	

Notes for Home: Your child learned about the wildlife and resources of the Southeast.
Home Activity: With your child, examine food resources from the Southeast, such as peanuts, rice, and citrus fruits, and discuss how your family and community depend on these resources.

© Scott Foresman 4

Vocabulary Review

Directions: Write the letter of the correct definition beside each vocabulary term.
You may use your textbook.

____ **1.** hurricane season

____ **2.** pulp

____ **3.** barrier islands

____ **4.** extinct

____ **5.** fossil fuel

____ **6.** wetlands

____ **7.** endangered species

____ **8.** fall line

____ **9.** hurricane

____ **10.** key

a. islands formed from deposits of sand and mud

b. marks the boundary between the Piedmont and the coastal plains

c. fuel that is formed in the earth from the remains of plants or animals

d. period from June to the beginning of November when hurricanes usually occur

e. combination of ground-up wood chips, water, and chemicals

f. low island

g. lands that are at times covered with water

h. violent storm that forms over the ocean

i. no longer existing

j. kind of animal or plant that is thought to be dying out

Notes for Home: Your child learned the vocabulary terms for Chapter 6.
Home Activity: Call out the vocabulary terms to your child in random order. As you say each term, have your child spell it and use it in an original sentence.

Vocabulary Preview

Directions: Circle the word that best completes each sentence. You may use your glossary.

1. A system of trains and buses that carry many people through a city is a (Trail of Tears, public transportation system).

2. Many Southern states decided to (secede, consensus), or pull out, from the United States when Abraham Lincoln won the presidency.

3. The Cherokee's journey from the Southeast to what is now Oklahoma is known as the (Reconstruction, Trail of Tears).

4. (Pioneers, Civil rights) include the right to vote and to have the protection of the law.

5. In the past, you might have expected to find slaves on a (plantation, segregation) in the Southeast.

6. A (backwoodsman, pioneer) is a person who lived in a forest far away from towns.

7. The Northern states in the Civil War were called the (Union, Confederacy).

8. The Southern states in the Civil War formed a group called the (Union, Confederacy).

9. A person who settled in a part of a country and prepared it for others was a (slave, pioneer).

10. The (Civil War, civil rights) began in 1861 and pitted U.S. citizens against each other.

11. To separate black people and white people in public places is to (segregate, Confederacy) them.

12. Before making a decision, the Cherokee first had to reach a (Civil War, consensus).

13. (Segregation, Reconstruction) was the period of time after the Civil War when the South's buildings and economy were rebuilt.

14. In 1828 people rushed to Dahlonega, Georgia, during the first (gold rush, plantation) in the United States.

© Scott Foresman 4

Notes for Home: Your child learned the vocabulary terms for Chapter 7.
Home Activity: Use the vocabulary terms to create a crossword puzzle for your child. Use the definitions as clues for each term in the puzzle.

Lesson 1: The Cherokee

Directions: Read each of the following phrases. Number them from 1 (earliest) to 8 (most recent) to show the order in which they occurred.

_____ The United States government forced the Cherokee to give up their land and move to what is now Oklahoma.

_____ Many Cherokee and other Native Americans became ill with diseases the Europeans brought.

_____ Traders and other settlers began moving onto Cherokee land.

_____ The Cherokee made their homes in the mountains of southern Appalachia.

_____ The United States government tried to end conflicts between the Cherokee and settlers.

_____ The Cherokee formed their own government and wrote a constitution that was similar to the United States Constitution.

_____ Spanish explorers traveled through the Southeast.

_____ Gold was discovered on Cherokee land.

Directions: Answer the following questions on the lines provided.

1. What did Sequoyah contribute to the Cherokee? How was his contribution beneficial to others?

_____

_____

_____

2. How was the Cherokee constitution similar to the U.S. Constitution?

_____

_____

_____

Notes for Home: Your child learned about the Cherokee in the Southeast.
Home Activity: With your child, discuss how settlers and the Cherokee might have found a more constructive way to resolve their conflicts over land. Ask your child how he or she might apply this principle to conflicts in his or her own life.

Name _____ Date _____

Lesson 2: Early History of the Southeast

Directions: The box below contains the names of people and places that were very important to the early history of the Southeast. Match one name from the box with each label on the time line. You may use your textbook.

George Washington	Hernando de Soto	St. Augustine
Andrew Jackson	Roanoke Island	Juan Ponce de León
Jamestown, Virginia	Thomas Jefferson	Robert de La Salle

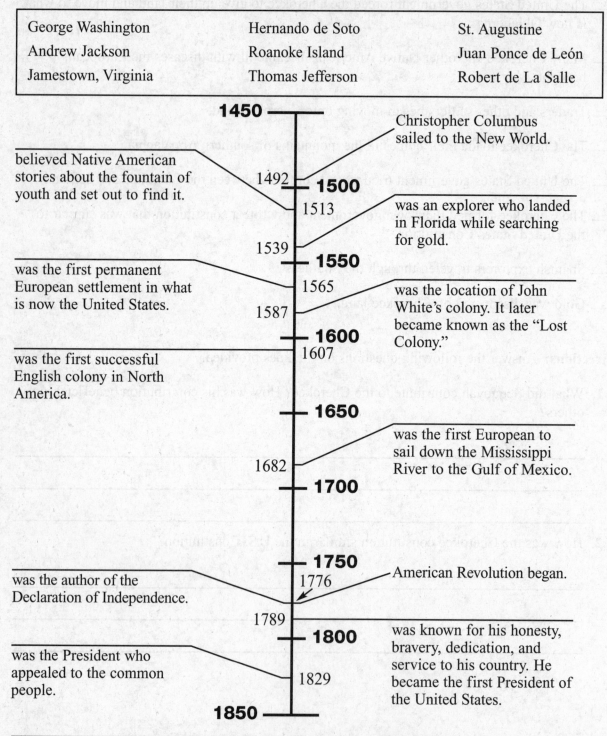

1450

Christopher Columbus sailed to the New World.

believed Native American stories about the fountain of youth and set out to find it.

1492

1500

1513

was an explorer who landed in Florida while searching for gold.

1539

1550

was the first permanent European settlement in what is now the United States.

1565

was the location of John White's colony. It later became known as the "Lost Colony."

1587

1600

1607

was the first successful English colony in North America.

1650

was the first European to sail down the Mississippi River to the Gulf of Mexico.

1682

1700

1750

American Revolution began.

1776

was the author of the Declaration of Independence.

1789

1800

was known for his honesty, bravery, dedication, and service to his country. He became the first President of the United States.

was the President who appealed to the common people.

1829

1850

© Scott Foresman 4

Notes for Home: Your child learned about the early history of the Southeast.
Home Activity: With your child, discuss what each of the early explorers of the Southeast originally set out to do. Did the explorers achieve their goals? What did they accomplish?

Lesson 3: The Nation Divided

Directions: Read each phrase below. Then decide whether the phrase refers to the North or the South during the Civil War. If it refers to the North, write an *N* on the line beside the statement. If it refers to the South, write an *S*. If it refers to both, write a *B*. You may use your textbook.

_____ 1. location of Fort Sumter

_____ 2. fought over Fort Sumter

_____ 3. called itself the Union

_____ 4. formed the Confederate States of America

_____ 5. had strong opinions about slavery

_____ 6. thought that each state should have more control over what its citizens could do

_____ 7. thought that the national government should have more power

_____ 8. seceded from the United States

_____ 9. did not want slavery to be allowed in the new states added to the nation

_____ 10. thought slavery should be allowed in the new states

_____ 11. surrendered after four years of fighting

_____ 12. won the war

_____ 13. suffered the loss of many lives during the war

_____ 14. one in four soldiers died in the war

_____ 15. underwent Reconstruction after the Civil War

_____ 16. enforced "Jim Crow" laws

_____ 17. tried to return their lives to normal after the war

_____ 18. did not allow slavery after the war

Notes for Home: Your child learned about the Civil War and its effects on the Southeast.
Home Activity: With your child, discuss how the United States would be affected if the North and South went to war today. How might your family be affected?

Identify Fact and Opinion

A *fact* is a statement that can be checked and proved to be true. An *opinion* tells about personal feelings and cannot be proved to be true or false.

Directions: Read the following paragraph. Then answer the questions about facts and opinions.

Today is December 2, 1862. Mother, Father, and I have been in Washington, D.C., for almost one week now. We are very lucky to be here right now. Washington, D.C., must be the busiest city in the world! Yesterday, President Lincoln sent Congress a State of the Union Address. Father took me with him to listen as the address was read. It was amazing! In the address, the President said that if his new plan is passed, it will shorten the war. I think that would be wonderful.

1. What are two facts from the paragraph? How do you know these are facts?

   _____

   _____

   _____

2. What are two opinions from the paragraph? How do you know these are opinions?

   _____

   _____

   _____

Notes for Home: Your child learned to distinguish between fact and opinion.
Home Activity: With your child, find a newspaper or magazine article about a current event. Discuss which parts of the article are facts and which parts are opinions.

Lesson 4: The Glittering Cities

Directions: Use the terms in the box to complete each sentence with information from Lesson 4. You may use your textbook.

Dahlonega	Southeast	Triangle Region
Dahlonega Courthouse	Myrtle Beach	Raleigh
Atlanta	Naples	Durham
railroad center	Orlando	Chapel Hill
	Charleston	

1. The cities of the _____ are among the fastest growing in the United States. These cities include _____, South Carolina, and _____ and _____, Florida.

2. Atlanta started as a _____ in 1837.

3. A fast-growing center for research in medicine, computers, and other industries is the _____ of North Carolina.

4. The _____ is made of bricks that contain gold.

5. In _____, South Carolina, you can go to the South Carolina Aquarium and see plants and animals from all areas of the state.

6. The dome of Georgia's state capitol in _____ is made partially from gold that the people of Dahlonega gave to the state.

7. The Triangle Region of North Carolina is made up of the cities of _____, _____, and _____.

8. In 1828, gold was found in _____, a town in a mountain area in northern Georgia.

Notes for Home: Your child learned about the growing cities of the Southeast.
Home Activity: With your child, review the reasons for population growth in the Southeast. Then discuss what features might attract people to your city or community.

Name _____ Date _____

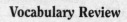

Vocabulary Review

Directions: Write the definition of each vocabulary term below on the lines provided. You may use your glossary.

1. consensus _____

_____

2. Trail of Tears _____

3. pioneer _____

_____

4. backwoodsman _____

5. plantation _____

6. slave _____

_____

7. Civil War _____

_____

8. Union _____

9. Confederacy _____

10. secede _____

11. Reconstruction _____

12. civil rights _____

_____

13. segregation _____

14. gold rush _____

_____

15. public transportation system _____

_____

 Notes for Home: Your child learned the vocabulary terms for Chapter 7.
Home Activity: With your child, make flash cards of the vocabulary terms by writing the term on one side of an index card and the definition on the other side. Then show your child one side of each card and have him or her supply the missing word or definition.

© Scott Foresman 4

UNIT 3 Project   This Just In

Use with Page 222.

Directions: Hold a classroom press conference about an important event in your state's history.

1. Our historic event is _____.

2. My role in the news conference (✔ one): ____government official ____expert

   ____news reporter ____eyewitness ____event participant

3. These are the most important details of the event:

   #1 _____

   #2 _____

   Outcome: _____

4. These are questions and answers about the event:

   Question: _____

   Answer: _____

   Question: _____

   Answer: _____

5. This is a description of our poster: _____

   _____

✔ Checklist for Students

_____ We chose a historic event.

_____ We assigned roles for the press conference.

_____ We wrote details of the event.

_____ We wrote questions and answers.

_____ We made a poster to announce the event.

_____ We presented our press conference.

Notes for Home: Your child learned how to report breaking news about an important event in your state's history.

Home Activity: With your child, watch a local or national press conference or news program. Discuss details about the reported events, roles of the participants in the program, and features included in the visuals used.

Cause and Effect

Directions: Very often an effect can have more than one cause. Fill in the circle
next to the correct answer.

1. Which word is NOT a cause-and-effect clue word?

   Ⓐ so
   Ⓑ both
   Ⓒ since
   Ⓓ because

2. Look at the organizer below. Which statement is the effect?

   Ⓐ The Midwest is connected by water to the Atlantic Ocean and much of the United
      States.
   Ⓑ The Midwest has rich farmland.
   Ⓒ The Midwest is in the middle of the country.
   Ⓓ The Midwest is a very important region of the United States.

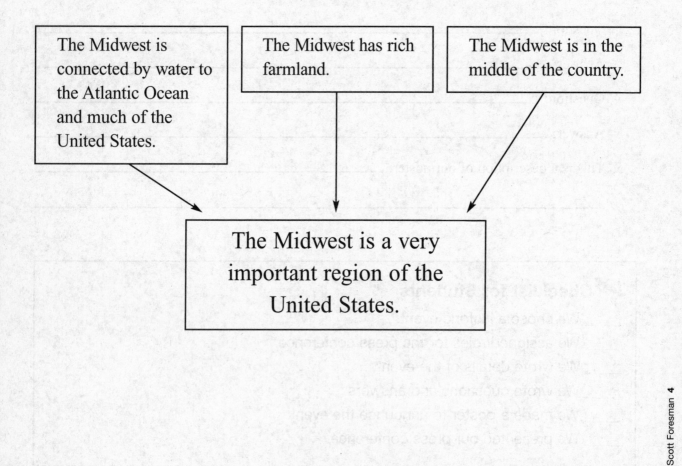

Notes for Home: Your child learned to determine causes and effects.
Home Activity: Discuss with your child the region of the United States where you live. Where is it located
in relation to the Midwest? Can you reach the Midwest easily from where you live? How could you get
there?

Vocabulary Preview

Directions: These are the vocabulary words from Chapter 8. How much do you know about them? Write the letter of each word's definition on the line at left. You may use your glossary.

_____ **1.** waterway

a. region of dry hills and sharp cliffs formed of crumbling rock

_____ **2.** canal

b. flat-bottomed boat

_____ **3.** lock

c. area where grasses grow well, but trees are rare

_____ **4.** barge

d. system of rivers, lakes, and canals through which many ships travel

_____ **5.** badlands

e. process of bringing water to farms to spray over fields

_____ **6.** erosion

f. the planting of different crops in different years

_____ **7.** prairie

g. waterway that has been dug across land for ships to go through

_____ **8.** crop rotation

h. process by which water and wind wear away rock

_____ **9.** irrigation

i. gated part of a canal or a river

Notes for Home: Your child learned the vocabulary terms for Chapter 8.
Home Activity: Discuss with your child any *canals, badlands,* or *prairies* you may have visited or seen in pictures, on television, or in movies.

Lesson 1: A Route to the Sea

The Great Lakes connect the Midwest region to other waterways around the world.

Directions: Use the waterways from this lesson to complete each sentence. Then answer the questions that follow. You may use your textbook.

1. The Great Lakes include Lake _____, Lake _____, Lake _____, Lake _____, and Lake _____.

2. The _____ connects Lake Michigan to the largest river in the United States. That river is the _____ River.

3. The _____ links the Great Lakes with the _____ River. That river flows into the _____ Ocean.

4. Many of the goods from the Midwest travel by barge and boat from the Great Lakes to the _____ Ocean.

Directions: Answer the following questions on the lines provided.

5. What are the disadvantages of shipping goods by barge?

   _____

   _____

   _____

6. What are the advantages of shipping goods by barge?

   _____

   _____

   _____

Notes for Home: Your child learned how waterways allow the goods of the Midwest to be sent all over the world.
Home Activity: Help your child map the Illinois Waterway. Have him or her list the bodies of water in order from west to east.

Compare Line and Bar Graphs

Line graphs show changes over time. Bar graphs also can show changes over time, or they can compare amounts.

Directions: Read the information in the box and create a line or bar graph to show the facts in a clear, simple picture. Choose the type of graph that best displays this type of information.

Farming is very important to many Midwestern states. Illinois is one state in which many different crops are grown. The following figures give the approximate number of Illinois farms that grew certain crops in a recent year: corn (for grain), 46,000; hay (along with silage and field seeds), 10,000; oats, 2,000; soybeans, 47,000; wheat, 15,000.

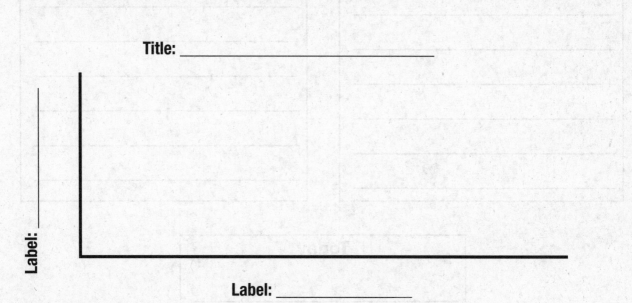

Title: _____

Label: _____

Label: _____

Directions: Answer the following questions about the graph you created.

1. What type of graph did you use to show the information? Why?

_____

_____

2. What information did you plot on the y axis?

_____

3. What information did you plot on the x axis?

_____

Notes for Home: Your child learned how to use line graphs and bar graphs.
Home Activity: Ask your child to think about the number of hours he or she spends each day on various activities, such as going to school, playing, and helping at home. Help your child create a line or bar graph to illustrate that information.

Lesson 2: The Badlands of South Dakota

Many years of erosion have created the Badlands of South Dakota. The changes that have taken place there have been dramatic.

Directions: Write a description of the Badlands in each of the boxes below. Include information about the types of plants and animals that have lived there. You may use your textbook.

Millions of Years Ago

_____

_____

_____

_____

_____

_____

Changes That Occurred Over Time

_____

_____

_____

_____

_____

_____

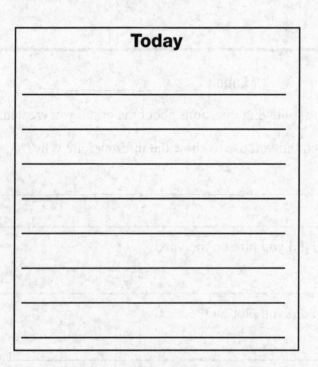

Today

_____

_____

_____

_____

_____

_____

_____

Notes for Home: Your child learned about the changes in the landscape that created the Badlands of South Dakota.
Home Activity: Discuss with your child how this type of landscape, *badlands*, might have received its name.

Lesson 3: Bountiful Midwestern Farms

The Midwest is an important farming region for the United States and the rest of the world.

Directions: Complete the chart with information about the many crops of the Midwest region. You may use your textbook.

Crop	Where Is It Grown?	Why Is It Grown There?
Wheat		
Sunflowers		
Corn		
Soybeans		
Oats		
Barley		
Hogs		
Cattle		

Notes for Home: Your child learned about the variety of crops and livestock grown in the Midwest region of the United States.
Home Activity: Discuss the products your family uses that might have come from crops grown in the Midwest.

Vocabulary Review

Directions: Use the clues from the chapter to complete the crossword puzzle.

waterway	lock	badlands	prairie	irrigation
canal	barge	erosion	crop rotation	

Across

2. gated part of a canal or river

6. region of dry hills and sharp cliffs formed of crumbling rock

8. process of bringing water to farms to spray over fields

9. system of rivers, lakes, and canals through which many ships travel

Down

1. the planting of different crops in different years

3. waterway that has been dug across land for ships to go through

4. process by which water and wind wear away rock

5. area where grasses grow well, but trees are rare

7. flat-bottomed boat

Notes for Home: Your child learned the vocabulary terms for Chapter 8.
Home Activity: Choose a few of the vocabulary words for your child to use in original sentences.

© Scott Foresman 4

Vocabulary Preview

Directions: These are the vocabulary words from Chapter 9. How much do you know about these words? Write each word on the line provided beside its definition. You may use your glossary.

fur trade	sod	mound	transcontinental railroad
mission	drought	steamboat	interstate highway system
trading post	Dust Bowl	hub	

1. _____ grass, roots, and dirt that form the ground's top layer

2. _____ set of wide, fast, interconnecting highways to link the states

3. _____ the exchange of animal skins for other goods, such as cloth, guns, and knives

4. _____ boat powered by a steam engine

5. _____ time of little rain

6. _____ rail line that crosses the entire country

7. _____ settlement set up by a religious group to teach its religion and to help the people of an area.

8. _____ area in the Midwest and Southwest that suffered the most during the drought in the 1930s

9. _____ center of activity

10. _____ type of store at which goods are traded

11. _____ pile of earth or stones

Notes for Home: Your child learned the vocabulary terms for Chapter 9.
Home Activity: Discuss with your child any of the terms above that may be related to your community today or in the past. For example, does the interstate highway system run through your community?

© Scott Foresman 4

Lesson 1: The Ojibwa

The Ojibwa have been an important part of the culture of the Midwest for many years.

Directions: Write details about the Ojibwa in each box of the idea web below. You may use your textbook.

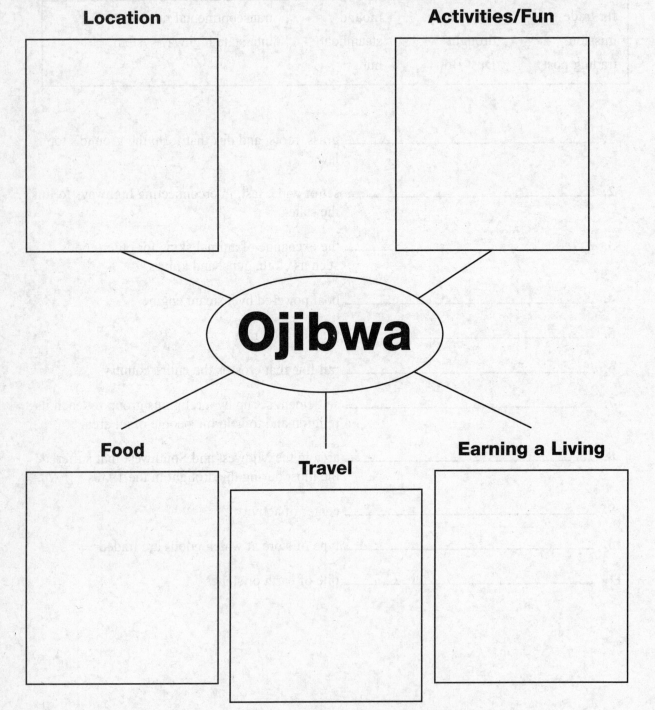

Location

Activities/Fun

Ojibwa

Food

Travel

Earning a Living

Notes for Home: Your child learned about the history of the Ojibwa.
Home Activity: Find out which Native American groups live or have lived near your community. Discuss with your child how these groups' cultures have influenced life in your community.

Use a Search Engine on the Internet

A search engine is a good tool to help you find information on the Internet. Using keywords allows you to narrow your search. Suppose that you are given the assignments that follow. Which keywords would you choose to research your task?

Directions: Circle the letter of the keyword or words that would best help you find information for each project below.

1. Plan an Ojibwa celebration for your classmates.

   a. Ojibwa   **b.** Ojibwa celebration   **c.** classmates

2. Write a paragraph about the northern Great Lakes region.

   a. paragraph   **b.** northern regions   **c.** northern Great Lakes region

3. Draw a map showing the Native American reservations in the United States.

   a. U.S. reservations   **b.** draw a map   **c.** maps

4. Make a model of an Ojibwa birchbark canoe.

   a. make a canoe   **b.** birchbark models   **c.** Ojibwa culture and travel

5. Write a report about the American Indian Movement.

   a. American Indian Movement   **b.** writing   **c.** report

Directions: Suppose you need to research the Midwest for a social studies presentation on this region. You plan to use a search engine to help you find information. On the lines below, list keywords you might use to research your task.

_____   _____

_____   _____

Notes for Home: Your child learned how to use a search engine on the Internet.
Home Activity: Does your child have access to the Internet at home, at school, or at a local library? Discuss any rules you have for your child's Internet use.

© Scott Foresman 4

Use with Pages 264–266.

Lesson 2: The Fur Trade

Many of the cities and towns of the Midwest began because of the fur trade.

Directions: Sequence the following events in the history of the fur trade in the order in which they took place. Number the events from 1 (earliest) to 10 (most recent). You may use your textbook.

_____ The French came to the Midwest.

_____ Marquette and Jolliet returned north to a mission at Green Bay.

_____ The French began building forts and using them as trading posts.

_____ The Ojibwa settled in the Midwest.

_____ Native Americans and the French began trapping beaver, mink, and otter.

_____ Native Americans began to settle and farm around the French forts.

_____ Jacques Marquette and Louis Jolliet traveled from Mackinaw in present-day Michigan to the Mississippi River.

_____ Jolliet settled as a fur trader in Sault Sainte Marie.

_____ Communities began to grow around the French forts.

_____ Sault St. Marie and Chicago grew into major cities.

Directions: On a separate sheet of paper, trace the map on page 265 of your textbook. Label the rivers and waterways mentioned in Lesson 2. Highlight Marquette and Jolliet's journey on your map.

© Scott Foresman 4

Notes for Home: Your child learned about the history of fur trade in the Midwest.
Home Activity: Trapping animals and wearing clothing made of animal fur are controversies today. Discuss with your child the advantages and disadvantages of fur trapping and trading as an industry.

Use with Pages 268–269.

Writing Prompt: Trading Long Ago and Today

Long ago, the English traded with Native Americans for furs. Trading helped both groups get the things they needed. Today, people still trade to get the things they need or want. Draw a picture of something you have traded and what you received in return. Write two sentences telling why you decided to make the trade.

Notes for Home: Your child learned about trading in colonial times.
Home Activity: With your child, discuss the ways in which trading helps people get the things they need or want.

Lesson 3: Building Farms

As settlers began to farm in the Midwest, the land changed.

Directions: Use complete sentences to answer the questions that follow. You may use your textbook.

1. What happened to the Native Americans who had once lived in Wapello County?

_____

_____

2. How did the American settlers in the Midwest claim their land?

_____

_____

3. Describe the two types of Midwestern farmhouses in the 1800s.

_____

_____

_____

_____

_____

4. What were the advantages and disadvantages of a sod house?

_____

_____

_____

5. Why was John Deere important to Midwestern farmers?

_____

_____

 Notes for Home: Your child learned about the beginnings of farming in the Midwest.
Home Activity: Discuss with your child the challenges faced by the Native Americans and the early farmers who lived in the Midwest. What character traits might have been important for both of these groups to have?

Lesson 4: Hub of the Nation

The Midwest has long been a center of trade and transportation for the United States.

Directions: Complete the chart with details from the lesson that support each main idea. You may use your textbook.

Main Idea	Supporting Details
Cahokia was once a key trading center in the Midwest.	
President Thomas Jefferson wanted to expand trade.	
One of the main reasons that St. Louis grew quickly was the invention of steamboats.	
Chicago began to rival St. Louis as the center of trade in the Midwest.	
The interstate highway system is very important to the United States.	

Notes for Home: Your child learned how the Midwest has served as the hub of the United States throughout much of our nation's history.
Home Activity: Look at a highway map of the United States. Which highways that pass through or nearby your community lead to the Midwest?

© Scott Foresman 4

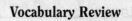
Vocabulary Review

Directions: Draw a picture to represent each of the vocabulary terms below. Then write the definition of each word on the lines that follow.

1. fur trade _____
   _____
   _____
   _____

2. mission _____
   _____
   _____
   _____
   _____

3. sod _____
   _____
   _____
   _____
   _____

4. mound _____
   _____
   _____
   _____
   _____

5. transcontinental railroad _____
   _____
   _____
   _____
   _____

6. interstate highway system _____
   _____
   _____
   _____

Notes for Home: Your child learned the vocabulary terms for Chapter 9.
Home Activity: With your child, take turns using each of the vocabulary words from Chapter 9 in an original sentence.

© Scott Foresman 4

UNIT 4 Project   Point of View

Use with Page 290.

Directions: In a group, debate two sides of an event or topic in your state's history.

1. Our debate topic is _____.

2. Here are two points of view and facts to support each side:

Pro: _____

Facts: _____

_____

_____

_____

Con: _____

Facts: _____

_____

_____

_____

3. _____ will give the Pro argument.

4. _____ will give the Con argument.

5. The class chose the _____ argument as the best presentation.

✔ Checklist for Students

_____ We chose a topic to debate.

_____ We identified two sides of the topic.

_____ We wrote facts to support two sides of the topic.

_____ We decided who will argue each side.

_____ We held our debate for the class.

Notes for Home: Your child learned how to defend a point of view.
Home Activity: Identify a topic of interest at home and two opposing points of view. With your child, debate the issue to support your position. Which side of the discussion presents the best supporting information?

Draw Conclusions

A conclusion is a decision you reach after you think about certain facts or details.

Directions: Read the facts. Answer the questions that follow. Fill in the circle next to the correct answer.

1. The Grand Canyon is a national park. There are many trails to hike on and activities to do there. There also are many hotels and restaurants located near the Grand Canyon. On the basis of these facts, what conclusion can you draw about the Grand Canyon?

   Ⓐ The Anasazi lived on the Colorado Plateau.
   Ⓑ The Grand Canyon was formed by erosion.
   Ⓒ The Havasupai still live at the bottom of the canyon.
   Ⓓ Many people visit the Grand Canyon each year.

2. The saguaro is a special cactus. It can only be found in the Sonoran Desert. This desert is located in Saguaro National Park in Arizona, where the climate is hot and dry. What conclusion can you draw about the saguaro on the basis of these facts?

   Ⓐ The saguaro does not need much water to live.
   Ⓑ The saguaro grows from a tiny, black seed.
   Ⓒ The saguaro has become a symbol of the Southwest.
   Ⓓ The saguaro can grow to over 40 feet tall.

3. Pattillo Higgins saw gas bubbles in a stream near Spindletop Hill in Texas. He thought that if there was gas underground, there might be oil, too. He tried to drill for oil at Spindletop. What conclusion can you draw about Pattillo Higgins on the basis of these facts?

   Ⓐ He did not find oil at Spindletop.
   Ⓑ He was a famous geologist.
   Ⓒ He was a smart and curious man.
   Ⓓ He liked to fish in streams.

Notes for Home: Your child learned to draw conclusions from a set of facts.
Home Activity: Share with your child a set of facts about activities that various family members enjoy. Help your child draw conclusions based on those facts.

© Scott Foresman 4

Vocabulary Preview

Directions: These are the vocabulary words from Chapter 10. How much do you know about these words? Write the number of each term on the line next to its definition. You may use your glossary.

1. adobe

2. pueblo

3. arid

4. savanna

5. gusher

6. refinery

_____ **a.** an oil well that produces a large amount of oil

_____ **b.** a climate that is dry, but is not a desert climate

_____ **c.** a factory that separates crude oil into different groups of chemicals

_____ **d.** mud brick

_____ **e.** "village" in Spanish

_____ **f.** a grassy plain on which few trees grow, with a hot and seasonally dry climate

Directions: Write the vocabulary word that best completes each sentence. Write the word on the line provided.

7. Some parts of the Southwest have an _____ climate because these areas might go a long time without rain.

8. The separation of crude oil into different groups of chemicals happens at

an oil _____ .

Notes for Home: Your child learned the vocabulary terms for Chapter 10.
Home Activity: Discuss the term *landform* with your child. Share examples of landforms from your community and the surrounding area.

Lesson 1: A Land of Canyons

The Grand Canyon is one of the most amazing landforms in the United States.

Directions: Suppose that you are going to write an article about the Grand Canyon for your school newspaper. Complete the chart below to help you get started. You may use your textbook.

The Grand Canyon

HOW was it formed?	
WHO first lived there? WHAT were their lives like?	
WHO still lives there?	
WHO explored there?	
WHO helped it become a tourist attraction? HOW?	
WHAT can you do there today?	

Notes for Home: Your child learned about the history of the Grand Canyon.
Home Activity: Has your family ever visited a national park? Perhaps you have been to the Grand Canyon. Discuss with your child any national parks that you have visited or would like to visit.

© Scott Foresman 4

Make Generalizations

A generalization is a statement that applies to many examples. It explains how many facts have one idea in common.

Directions: Read the following journal entries from a student who recently visited the Grand Canyon. Answer the questions below. Fill in the circle next to the correct answer.

Saturday, July 9

Mom and I left our apartment in Phoenix at 8 A.M. The drive seemed to take forever! When we arrived at the South Rim around noon, I was stunned by the canyon's magnificent views. The temperature was a hot 90 degrees!

Sunday, July 10

Today we took a mule ride down into the canyon. We could have also hiked or taken a helicopter to reach the bottom. The mule ride led us to the Colorado River at the canyon's floor. We saw people riding rafts on the river. We also saw campers trout fishing in it. The temperature really cooled off at dusk.

Monday, July 11

After spending the night at Phantom Ranch, a lodge on the canyon floor, we explored the site of an ancient Native American village. A park ranger then took us on a tour to learn about the different types of wildlife in the canyon.

1. Which of the following statements is a true generalization?

   Ⓐ Mom and I left our apartment at 8 A.M.
   Ⓑ There are several ways to reach the floor of the Grand Canyon.
   Ⓒ We arrived at the South Rim by noon.
   Ⓓ We saw campers trout fishing in the Colorado River.

2. Which of the following statements is a true generalization?

   Ⓐ On Saturday, the temperature was a hot 90 degrees.
   Ⓑ On Sunday, the temperature really cooled off at dusk.
   Ⓒ The temperature varies in the Grand Canyon.
   Ⓓ We explored the site of an ancient Native American village.

3. Write a generalization based on the following facts. Write your answer on the lines provided.

   • Phantom Ranch is located at the bottom of the Grand Canyon.
   • An ancient Native American village is located at the bottom of the Grand Canyon.
   • Park rangers give tour guides at the bottom of the Grand Canyon.

   _____

   _____

Notes for Home: Your child learned how to make generalizations.
Home Activity: With your child, take turns inventing sentences that begin with "Generally," or "Generally speaking."

Lesson 2: Climates in the Southwest

Much of the Southwest has a hot, dry climate.

Directions: Using information from this lesson, circle the term in parentheses that best completes each sentence. You may use your textbook.

1. A desert is an area that gets less than (ten, five) inches of rain each year.

2. Some parts of the Southwest have an (arid, icy) climate but are not deserts.

3. The eastern part of (Colorado, Texas) has a hot, humid climate.

4. (Oklahoma, New Mexico) can sometimes have a humid and windy climate.

5. Thunderstorms, blizzards, and tornadoes are caused when (wet, cold) and warm air masses meet.

6. Thunderstorms, blizzards, and (tornadoes, hurricanes) are possible in Oklahoma.

7. The saguaro is a kind of cactus that grows naturally in the (Sonoran Desert, Central Plain).

8. The saguaro's white, night-blooming blossom is (Oklahoma's, Arizona's) state flower.

9. To grow big and strong, the saguaro spreads its (roots, flowers) to drink in the rainwater.

10. The cactus can store enough (food, water) to keep alive through long, dry periods.

11. The saguaro provides shelter for desert (plants, animals).

12. Some trees grow in a savanna, but most of the plants growing here are (cactuses, grasses).

13. Piñon pines and junipers grow in the (savannas, deserts) of the Southwest.

© Scott Foresman 4

Notes for Home: Your child learned about the climates of the Southwest region.
Home Activity: Discuss with your child the climate of your community. How is it similar to or different from the climates in the Southwest region?

Lesson 3: Oil and Technology

For many years, the Southwest has been a leader in research and discovery.

Directions: Complete the outline with information from this lesson. You may use your textbook.

Research and Discovery in the Southwest

I. The Discovery of Oil

    A. Many people went to _____ in search of oil and natural gas.

    B. _____ became an important oil town.

    C. Pattillo Higgins

        1. was a businessman and _____.

        2. thought there might be _____ beneath _____.

        3. hired _____ to drill the gusher.

    D. Oil

        1. comes out of the ground as a thick, black liquid called _____.

        2. is separated in a _____.

        3. can be used in products such as _____, _____,

        _____, _____, _____,

        _____, and _____.

        4. is a _____ resource, or one that cannot be replaced by nature.

II. Technology in the Southwest

    A. Arizona companies manufacture _____,

    _____, _____, and _____.

    B. _____'s researchers study medicine, genetics, and telecommunications.

    C. Texas companies make _____, _____,

    _____, and _____.

    D. _____ companies assist the electronic, aviation, and space industries.

Notes for Home: Your child learned about some of the research and discoveries that have taken place in the Southwest.
Home Activity: Many products are made from oil. Which of the products listed and pictured in your child's textbook do you use? Do you know of any others that your family uses? Discuss these with your child.

© Scott Foresman 4

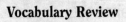

Vocabulary Review

Directions: Use each of the vocabulary terms from Chapter 10 in a sentence. Write the sentences on the lines provided. You may use your glossary.

1. adobe

_____

_____

2. pueblo

_____

_____

3. arid

_____

_____

4. savanna

_____

_____

5. refinery

_____

_____

6. gusher

_____

_____

 Notes for Home: Your child learned the vocabulary terms for Chapter 10.
Home Activity: Choose one of the terms from this chapter. Take turns with your child using the term in a sentence. See how many sentences you can create!

© Scott Foresman 4

Name _____ Date _____

Vocabulary Preview

Directions: These are the vocabulary words from Chapter 11. How much do you know about these words? Write each word in the space beside its meaning. You may use your glossary.

hogan	missionary	tallow	aqueduct
viceroy	vaquero	homestead	

1. _____ governor

2. _____ Spanish cowboy

3. _____ one-room home of the Navajo

4. _____ trench or pipe used to bring water from a distance

5. _____ fat of cattle used for candles and soap

6. _____ person who is sent by a religious organization into other parts of the world to spread its beliefs

7. _____ land given to a settler

Directions: Use the following vocabulary words in an original sentence. Write your sentences on the lines provided.

8. hogan _____

_____

9. tallow _____

_____

 Notes for Home: Your child learned the vocabulary terms for Chapter 11.
Home Activity: Even today, aqueducts carry water to some communities. From where does your community receive its water supply? Discuss this with your child.

Lesson 1: The Navajo

The Navajo have lived in and been an important part of the Southwest for centuries.

Directions: Write the number for each term on the line next to its definition or description.

1. Diné
2. hogan
3. Kit Carson
4. Fort Canby

5. Bosque Redondo
6. "The Long Walk"
7. Navajo Tribal Council

8. Henry Chee Dodge
9. Navajo Nation
10. Window Rock

_____ the largest Native American group in the United States

_____ area in New Mexico to which the Navajo were forced to walk three hundred miles

_____ home made of logs and covered with a thick layer of soil

_____ army post in Arizona to which the Navajo were ordered to move

_____ in Arizona; the Navajo capital

_____ a soldier who was ordered by the U.S. government to stop conflicts between the Navajo and the white settlers in New Mexico

_____ "the people;" what Navajo people called themselves before European settlers came to North America

_____ first chairman of the Navajo Tribal Council

_____ the 300-mile journey to Bosque Redondo along which many Navajo died

_____ made the first written system of Navajo laws

Notes for Home: Your child learned about the history of the Navajo.
Home Activity: Discuss "The Long Walk" of the Navajo with your child. Together, brainstorm a list of reasons how the journey got its name.

Workbook

Identify Primary and Secondary Sources

As you research a particular topic, you can use primary and secondary sources for different purposes.

Directions: Read the descriptions below. Write whether each source is *primary* or *secondary* on the lines provided.

1. You have found an article in a magazine about life at the Grand Canyon written by a Havasupai. Is the article a primary or secondary source? _____

2. You are reading a biography of John Wesley Powell written by a historian. Is the book a primary or secondary source? _____

3. You have discovered a newspaper article describing a tornado in Oklahoma. It was written by an eyewitness to the storm. Is the article a primary or secondary source?

_____

4. You have found a letter written by Pattillo Higgins about his search for oil. Is the letter a primary or secondary source? _____

5. You are reading the section in your social studies textbook about Jerrie Cobb. Is the section a primary or secondary source? _____

6. You read an editorial in your newspaper written by a Navajo Native American. Is the editorial a primary or secondary source? _____

7. You found a biography about Henry Chee Dodge. Is it a primary or secondary source?

_____

Notes for Home: Your child learned how to distinguish between primary and secondary sources.
Home Activity: Find a newspaper or magazine article. Review it with your child. Is it a primary or secondary source? If it is a secondary source, are any eyewitnesses or participants quoted in it?

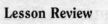

Lesson 2: Spanish Influence

The Spanish established their presence in the Southwest many years ago.

Directions: Complete the charts below with information from the lesson. You may use your textbook.

Spanish Influence in the Southwest

Francisco Vásquez de Coronado:	
WHAT was his goal?	
WHAT did he really do?	
WHAT happened when he went back to Mexico later?	

Missionaries:	
WHAT were their goals?	
WHAT did they really do?	
WHAT happened later?	

Notes for Home: Your child learned about Spanish influence in the Southwest United States.
Home Activity: Look at a map of the Southwest region, either in your child's textbook or in another source. Point out to your child places with Spanish names, such as *Santa Fe, New Mexico,* and *San Antonio, Texas.* Discuss with your child other Spanish place names.

Name _____ Date _____

Lesson 3: Ranches and Drivers

Cattle ranches can be found throughout the Southwest region.

Directions: Using information from this lesson, select a term in the box to complete each sentence. You may use your textbook.

Montana	tallow	Annie Oakley	Mexican
meat	Kansas	King	Philip Armour

1. Early Texas settlers raised cattle to use as _____ for their families.

2. The _____ of the cattle was used for candles and soap.

3. In 1870 _____ started a meat-packing industry in Chicago.

4. Cattle became important not only to the Southwest but also to northern states, such as

   _____ and the Dakotas.

5. In South Texas, many cowboys were of _____ descent.

6. _____ and Calamity Jane were famous cowgirls who performed in wild-west shows.

7. Many ranchers drove their cattle from Texas all the way to _____ on the Chisholm Trail.

8. The _____ Ranch spreads over 800,000 acres and is larger than the state of Rhode Island.

© Scott Foresman 4

Notes for Home: Your child learned about ranching in the Southwest.
Home Activity: Discuss with your child the importance of cattle ranching to families in your town. Also discuss the dairy industry.

Use with Pages 344–345.

Writing Prompt: Cowboys and Cowgirls

Driving cattle was an important and difficult job in the "Wild West." Think about what you have read about the cowboys and cowgirls of today and long ago. Write a paragraph about how modern cowhands' jobs are similar to and different from those of cowhands long ago.

_____

_____

_____

_____

_____

_____

_____

_____

_____

_____

_____

_____

_____

Notes for Home: Your child learned about cowhands today and long ago.
Home Activity: With your child, brainstorm jobs that people do now that they also did long ago, such as doctor or cook. Discuss how jobs today and long ago are similar and different.

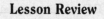
Lesson 4: Living in the Desert

Even though most of Arizona is a desert, large cities have been built there.

Directions: Suppose that you live in Phoenix, Arizona. Write a letter to a friend or family member who lives in another region. Describe life in the desert. Include information about inventions that have improved desert living. You may use your textbook.

Dear _____,

_____

_____

_____

_____

_____

_____

_____

_____

_____

_____

_____

_____

Sincerely yours,

_____

Notes for Home: Your child learned about living in a desert region.
Home Activity: Discuss air conditioning with your child. Does your family have it at home? If so, discuss the need to conserve energy by keeping the thermostat at a reasonable setting. If not, brainstorm with your child ways your family can keep cool during warm weather.

© Scott Foresman 4

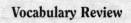
Vocabulary Review

Directions: Use the vocabulary words from Chapter 11 to complete the crossword puzzle.

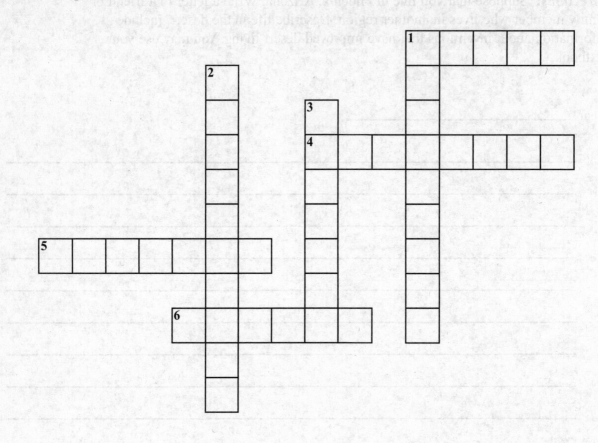

Across

1. one-room home of the Navajo

4. trench or pipe used to bring water from a distance

5. governor

6. fat of cattle used for candles and soap

Down

1. land given to a settler

2. person who is sent by a religious organization into other parts of the world to spread its beliefs

3. Spanish cowboy

Notes for Home: Your child learned the vocabulary terms for Chapter 11.
Home Activity: Some of the terms from this chapter come directly from other languages. For example, the word *aqueduct* comes from Latin. Have your child find the chapter vocabulary term that is in Spanish. Discuss with your child why the word for the first cowboys is Spanish.

Discovery CHANNEL SCHOOL

Use with Page 358.

UNIT 5 Project Ad Sales

Directions: In a group, make an infomercial to sell a product or business that helps your state's economy.

1. Our product or business is _____.

2. These are facts about our product or business:

_____

_____

_____

_____

_____

3. We wrote a script for our infomercial, including these topics:

_____history _____value or importance _____cost

_____success stories _____how it helps our state's economy

4. We made a poster or banner to use in our infomercial. This is the slogan we used in our advertisement:

_____

✔ Checklist for Students

_____ We chose a product or business.

_____ We wrote facts about the product or business.

_____ We wrote an infomercial script.

_____ We made an advertisement on a poster or banner.

_____ We presented our infomercial to the class.

Notes for Home: Your child made an infomercial to advertise a product or business.
Home Activity: With your child, make a chart of local businesses and the products and services they provide to your community. Discuss different ways in which businesses advertise their products to the community.

Compare and Contrast

Comparisons and contrasts often are used to tell how two or more things are alike and different.

Directions: Read the passage and use the reading strategy of compare and contrast to answer the questions below. Fill in the circle next to the correct answer.

There are many national parks in the United States. Two of them are Yellowstone National Park and Yosemite National Park. Yellowstone covers more than 2.2 million acres in parts of Idaho, Wyoming, and Montana. Yosemite covers more than 760,000 acres in an area of California called the Sierra Nevada.

Yellowstone and Yosemite are both known for their waterfalls, meadows, and forests. The forests of Yosemite also include hundreds of giant sequoias, the world's largest living trees. Yellowstone has thousands of hot springs and geysers.

A famous geyser, Old Faithful, is one of Yellowstone's biggest attractions.

Yosemite is famous for El Capitan, the largest single rock on earth. Rock climbers travel from all over the world to try to climb it. El Capitan was left standing when glaciers swept through the land long ago. In fact, much of both parks was formed when glaciers carved through sections of rock and covered the land. When the glaciers melted, the water formed lakes and valleys throughout the land.

1. How does Yosemite differ from Yellowstone?

   Ⓐ Yosemite has waterfalls, forests, and meadows.
   Ⓑ The forests of Yosemite include sequoias.
   Ⓒ Much of Yosemite was formed by glaciers.
   Ⓓ Yosemite has thousands of hot springs and geysers.

2. In what ways are the two parks alike?

   Ⓐ Both parks cover more than 2.2 million acres of land.
   Ⓑ Rock climbers travel from all over the world to try to climb El Capitan.
   Ⓒ Both parks have thousands of hot springs and geysers.
   Ⓓ Much of both parks was formed by glaciers.

Notes for Home: Your child learned how to compare and contrast printed information.
Home Activity: Help your child compare and contrast weekday activities and weekend activities. How do your child's weekdays compare and contrast with weekends?

Name _____ Date _____

Vocabulary Preview

Directions: Match each vocabulary term in the box to its meaning. Write the vocabulary term on the line provided. You may use your glossary.

timber line	lava	rain shadow
geyser	tundra	greenhouse
magma	frigid	livestock
volcano		reforest

1. _____ animals that are raised on farms and ranches

2. _____ form of molten rock that rises and flows on Earth's surface

3. _____ type of hot spring that erupts, shooting hot water into the air

4. _____ cold, flat area where trees cannot grow

5. _____ mountain with an opening through which ash, gas, and lava are forced

6. _____ place on a mountain above which no trees can grow

7. _____ enclosed structure that allows light to enter and keeps heat and moisture from escaping

8. _____ very cold

9. _____ process of planting new trees to replace those that have been cut

10. _____ condition of dryness that occurs on the eastern side of high coastal mountains

11. _____ large mass of molten rock within the ground that provides heat for geysers and hot springs

Notes for Home: Your child learned the vocabulary terms for Chapter 12.
Home Activity: With your child, make flash cards of the vocabulary terms. Have your child illustrate the term on one side of the card and write the term on the other side. As you show your child each picture, have him or her identify and define the corresponding term.

© Scott Foresman 4

Lesson 1: A Land of Mountains

Many people visit the Rocky Mountains and Yellowstone National Park to see their beauty and landscape.

Directions: Complete the chart with information from this lesson. Then answer the questions that follow. You may use your textbook.

	Rocky Mountains	**Yellowstone National Park**
What Is It?		
Where Is It Located?		
What Is Its Size?		
What Are Its Features?		
What Are Its Attractions?		

1. What are some of the animals that live in the mountains? In which areas of the mountains do they live?

   _____

   _____

   _____

   _____

2. What are some other mountain ranges located in the western United States?

   _____

   _____

 Notes for Home: Your child learned about mountain ranges and national parks located in the West region of the United States.
Home Activity: With your child, find out more about the Rocky Mountains or Yellowstone National Park. Use information from the lesson to help you make a list of things to do and sights to see there.

© Scott Foresman 4

Take Notes and Write Outlines

Taking notes can help you remember what you have read. Notes are bits of information you write in your own words. An outline is a way of organizing important information.

Directions: Read the paragraph below and take notes by writing important facts and details on the note card. Then use your notes to complete the outline.

Glacier

A glacier is a moving mass of ice that can survive for many years. Glaciers are formed in regions of high snowfall and freezing temperatures. With each new snowstorm, layers of snow build. The snow becomes compacted under the weight of each new layer. The layers slowly grow together to form a thickened mass of ice. As the ice gets thicker, it begins to move. The great weight of glacier ice causes it to flow down mountains, through valleys, across plains, and spread into the sea. Glaciers transform and reshape the landscape.

Note Card

Glacier

-
-
-
-

Outline

Glacier

I. What is a glacier?

    A. _____

    B. can survive for many years

II. How is a glacier formed?

    A. layers of snow build

    B. _____

        _____

    C. layers grow together to form mass of ice

III. What happens to a glacier?

    A. ice thickens and begins to move

    B. _____

        _____

Notes for Home: Your child learned how to take notes and make an outline.
Home Activity: With your child, take notes on a newspaper or magazine article of your choice. Then organize your notes in an outline. How are your notes and outline alike and different?

Lesson 2: Climates in the West

Directions: Read the following statements. Then write *T* (True) or *F* (False) on the line before each statement. If the answer is false, correct the underlined term or terms to make the statement true. You may use your textbook.

_____ 1. Of all the areas in the United States, parts of <u>Hawaii</u> have some of the coldest temperatures.

_____

_____ 2. At 20,320 feet, <u>Death Valley</u> is the highest peak in North America.

_____

_____ 3. Some parts of California and Hawaii <u>very rarely</u> have temperatures that drop below freezing.

_____

_____ 4. California is such a large state that it has <u>the same climate</u> in its different areas.

_____

_____ 5. Plants in the Great Basin need <u>large</u> amounts of water to survive.

_____

_____ 6. Many areas in the West are made up of <u>tundra</u>, <u>tropics</u>, or <u>deserts</u>.

_____

_____ 7. <u>Rainier Paradise Ranger Station in Washington</u> receives fewer than two inches of rain each year.

_____

_____ 8. <u>Mount McKinley</u> is the wettest place on Earth, with an average annual rainfall on the mountain of 460 inches.

_____

_____ 9. The reason for differences in precipitation between western and eastern sides of the Cascade Mountains is an effect called the <u>rain shadow</u>.

_____

Notes for Home: Your child learned about variations in the climates of the West.
Home Activity: With your child, compare and contrast the climate in which you live with the different climates in the West. Which climate in the West is most similar to the region in which you live?

© Scott Foresman 4

Lesson 3: Resources of the West

Directions: The first column of the chart below lists products that are produced in the West. Complete the second column of the chart by writing the state of the West that matches each description. You may use your textbook.

Agricultural Products	States
Producer of the widest variety of fruits, vegetables, and nuts	
Grows barley, oats, hay, and potatoes in a harsh climate	
Biggest producer of potatoes in U.S.	
Produces sugarcane, pineapples, macadamia nuts, and coffee in a tropical climate	
Famous for its apples but also grows cherries, pears, and potatoes	
More than 880 million dollars a year made in catching cod, flounder, salmon, crab, and shrimp	
Swordfish and tuna caught off the coast of the islands	

Notes for Home: Your child learned about food and other products provided by the West.
Home Activity: With your child, discuss how different states in the West are able to produce the resources for which they are known. How do climate and location affect what they are able to produce?

Vocabulary Review

Directions: Circle the vocabulary term that best completes each sentence. You may use your textbook.

1. Because the climate in most of Alaska is harsh, plants grown there often are grown in a (rain shadow, greenhouse).

2. A (glacier, tundra) is a cold, flat land area where trees cannot grow, and where some people enjoy cross-country skiing.

3. Areas east of the Cascade Mountains receive much less rain than other areas of the mountain because of an effect called the (rain shadow, timber line).

4. A large mass of molten rock, or (lava, magma), still lies beneath the surface of Yellowstone and provides heat for the park's geysers and hot springs.

5. Old Faithful, the most famous (greenhouse, geyser) at Yellowstone, erupts about every 45 to 110 minutes, sending a stream of boiling water into the air.

6. Because wood is an important part of our daily lives, timber companies usually (reforest, tundra) areas where they have cut the trees.

7. Cattle, sheep, and pigs are examples of (timber line, livestock), or animals that are raised on farms and ranches.

8. No trees can grow above the (volcano, timber line) of a mountain because temperatures are too cold.

9. When a volcano erupts, a form of molten rock called (lava, magma) comes out of the opening.

10. States such as Washington and Montana are accustomed to very cold, or (glacier, frigid), winter temperatures and heavy snowfall.

11. A (volcano, geyser) is a type of mountain that has an opening through which ash, gas, and lava are forced.

© Scott Foresman 4

Notes for Home: Your child learned the vocabulary terms for Chapter 12.
Home Activity: Create a crossword puzzle of the vocabulary terms in this chapter, using the definitions as clues for each term. Have your child complete the puzzle.

Name _____ Date _____

Vocabulary Preview

Directions: Match each vocabulary term on the left with its definition on the right. Write the letter of the definition on the line beside the term. You may use your textbook.

_____ **1.** totem pole

_____ **2.** potlatch

_____ **3.** prospector

_____ **4.** boom town

_____ **5.** ghost town

_____ **6.** computer software

_____ **7.** international trade

a. feast often held to celebrate important events in a family's life

b. programs that help computers run certain functions

c. fast-growing town located near the discovery of gold, silver or other valuable metal ore

d. trade between different countries

e. tall post carved with images of people and animals

f. town that was deserted once the metal ore in the area was mined

g. person who searches for valuable minerals

Directions: Imagine you are a prospector heading toward California in search of gold. Write a diary entry in which you describe your experiences on your journey to California. Use the terms *prospector, boom town,* and *ghost town* in your entry.

_____

_____

_____

_____

_____

_____

_____

Notes for Home: Your child learned the vocabulary terms for Chapter 13.
Home Activity: With your child, make a list of products you have at home and, by reading the labels, identify the countries in which they were made. Discuss international trade and some of the goods that are exchanged between countries.

Name _____ Date _____

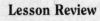
Lesson 1: The Tlingit

Directions: Use the terms in the box to complete each sentence with information from Lesson 1. Write the word on the line provided. You may use your textbook.

logging	money	gifts
fishing	Chilkat	trading network
potlatch	Sealaska Corporation	totem pole
Tlingit	household goods	

1. The _____ are a group of Native Americans who live along the southeastern coast of Alaska and the northern coast of British Columbia.

2. A Tlingit family often placed a _____, carved with images of people or animals, outside their home.

3. The Tlingit had a large _____ with other tribes through which they bought and sold canoes, copper, baskets, and other goods.

4. One of the most prized Tlingit products is a _____ blanket, which is woven from the dyed wool of mountain goats and sheep.

5. A Native American might hold a _____ to celebrate an important event such as a wedding, birth, or death.

6. During a traditional potlatch, the host gave _____ such as canoes, blankets, and other goods to each guest.

7. The gifts given at today's potlatches often include _____ and _____.

8. Today many Tlingit make their living by _____ or _____.

9. The _____ makes sure the Tlingit and other Native Americans will have enough money and land in the future.

Notes for Home: Your child learned about Native Americans called the Tlingit.
Home Activity: With your child, discuss what types of events occur at a traditional potlatch. Discuss reasons a potlatch might be held, the gifts that might be given, and the activities that might occur at a potlatch.

Workbook

Lesson 2: Exploration and Growth

Directions: Sequence the events in the order in which they took place by numbering them from 1 (earliest) to 13 (most recent). You may use your textbook.

_____ 1. The California Gold Rush begins.

_____ 2. Gold is found in Alaska.

_____ 3. Juan Rodríguez Cabrillo is probably the first European to see the coast of California.

_____ 4. American settlers travel to the West to claim California.

_____ 5. Hawaii becomes a state.

_____ 6. The Gold Rush ends, and many boom towns become ghost towns.

_____ 7. John Sutter and John Marshall discover gold in California, and word of the discovery gets out.

_____ 8. The cattle driving boom in the West begins.

_____ 9. The United States defeats Mexico, and Mexico is forced to give up California.

_____ 10. Alaska becomes a state.

_____ 11. Population in California soars, and businesses boom.

_____ 12. Russia sells Alaska to the United States for about two cents an acre.

_____ 13. The Franciscans build 21 missions in California.

Notes for Home: Your child learned about the history of the West.
Home Activity: With your child, discuss how the discovery of gold and other resources changed the West. How do these discoveries still affect the United States today?

Understand Latitude and Longitude

Directions: Use the terms in the box to complete each sentence. Write the terms on the line provided.

latitude	Northern Hemisphere	meridian	equator
parallel	Southern Hemisphere	prime meridian	longitude

1. Longitude is measured in degrees east and west of the _____.

2. Each _____, or line of latitude, is always the same distance

   apart from another.

3. The equator splits the Earth into two halves, called the _____

   and the _____.

4. A line that extends north and south is a line of _____.

5. A line that extends east and west is a line of _____.

6. Another name for a line of longitude is _____.

7. The _____ is the imaginary line, labeled 0° latitude, that

   divides Earth into two halves.

Directions: Answer the following questions on the lines provided. You may use your textbook.

8. What do lines of latitude and longitude form on globes and maps? _____

9. If a city is located on a line of latitude labeled 40°N, is it located in the Northern

   Hemisphere or Southern Hemisphere? _____

10. How does someone locate a place on a map by using its lines of latitude and longitude?

    _____

    _____

    _____

Notes for Home: Your child learned to use latitude and longitude to locate places on a map.
Home Activity: With your child, use the atlas map of the United States to find the approximate location of your city and other large cities in the United States.

© Scott Foresman 4

Lesson 3: Business and Pleasure

Directions: Classify each term or phrase by writing it in one of the city boxes below.

computer software, ships, jet airplanes	pleasant climate	second largest city in the United States
entertainment industry	California	skiing and winter sports
named after Great Salt Lake	high-tech companies	Space Needle
mining industry	Utah	movies and television shows
Washington	north of California	next to mountains

Los Angeles

1.   4.

2.

3.   5.

Seattle

1.   3.

                                          4.

2.   5.

Salt Lake City

1.   4.

2.   5.

3.

Notes for Home: Your child learned about businesses and attractions of cities in the West.
Home Activity: With your child, locate Los Angeles, Seattle, and Salt Lake City on a United States map. Then make a Venn diagram to compare and contrast the climate, attractions, and businesses located in these cities.

Vocabulary Review

Directions: The underlined vocabulary terms below have been misplaced so that each appears in the wrong sentence. Write each term on the line beside the sentence in which it actually belongs. You may use your textbook.

_____   **1.** A <u>potlatch</u> was a person looking for gold.

_____   **2.** Trade between the United States and countries that border the Pacific Ocean is called <u>computer software</u>.

_____   **3.** A town that sprang up due to the discovery of gold or silver in the area was called a <u>ghost town</u>.

_____   **4.** The figures on a <u>prospector</u> are carved and often brightly painted with images of people and animals.

_____   **5.** A <u>totem pole</u> is a traditional feast held by some Native Americans to celebrate important events in a family's life.

_____   **6.** A town often became a <u>boom town</u> once an area was mined and the town was deserted.

_____   **7.** Many high-tech companies that make <u>international trade</u> are located in Seattle, Washington.

Directions: In the box on the left, draw a picture of an 1800s boom town in the West. Then, in the box on the right, draw a picture to show what a boom town might have looked like when it became a ghost town.

Boom Town	**Ghost Town**

Notes for Home: Your child learned the vocabulary terms for Chapter 13.
Home Activity: With your child, practice saying, spelling, and using these vocabulary terms in correct contexts.

© Scott Foresman 4

Discovery CHANNEL SCHOOL

Use with Page 424.

UNIT
6 Project Great State

Directions: In a group, prepare a booklet that shows what's great about your state today—and what will be great in the future.

1. Our current event is _____.

2. This is a description of the current event:

_____

_____

_____

3. This is our prediction of what will happen in the future:

_____

_____

4. This is a description of the pictures we will include in our booklet:

1st picture: _____

2nd picture: _____

3rd picture: _____

4th picture: _____

✔ Checklist for Students

_____ We chose a current event about our state.

_____ We wrote a paragraph about the current event.

_____ We wrote predictions about the future.

_____ We illustrated the current event.

_____ We shared our booklet with the class.

Notes for Home: Your child learned about current events in your state.
Home Activity: With your child, discuss some events that occurred in the past in your state.
Share details about the event, and discuss how the event has affected your state today.

© Scott Foresman 4

NOTES

_____

_____

_____

_____

_____

_____

_____

_____

_____

_____

_____

_____

_____

_____

_____

_____

_____

_____

_____

_____

_____

_____

_____

_____

_____

NOTES

NOTES

NOTES

NOTES

NOTES

NOTES

NOTES

NOTES

NOTES